ANCIENT WARFARE

Publisher: Rolof van Hövell tot Westerflier
Editorial staff: Jasper Oorthuys (editor),
Eugene Harding (copy), Dirk van Gorp
Marketing and media manager: Christianne C. Beall

Contributors: Paul Bardunias, Duncan B. Campbell,
Seán Hussmann, Allison Kirk, Peter Krentz,
Jona Lendering, Paul McDonnell-Staff, Dan Powers,
Fred E. Ray, Owen Rees, Ronald Ruiters, Nicholas
Sekunda, Stefanos Skarmintzos, Natascha Sojc,
Michael J. Taylor, Marek Wozniak.
Illustrations: Giorgio Albertini, Jason Askew, Andrew
Brozyna, Dariusz Bufnal, Igor Dzis, Angel Garcia Pintó,
Carlos de la Rocha, Sebastian Schulz.

Design & layout: © MeSa Design.www.mesadesign.nl
e-mail: layout@ancient-warfare.com
Print: PublisherPartners. www.publisherpartners.com

Editorial office
PO Box 4082, 7200 BB Zutphen, The Netherlands.
Phone: +44-20-88168281 (Europe)
+1-740-994-0091 (US).
E-mail: editor@ancient-warfare.com
Skype: ancient_warfare
Website: www.ancient-warfare.com

Contributions in the form of articles, letters and queries
from readers are welcomed. Please send to the above
address or use the contact form on our website.

Subscription
Subscription price is 33.50 euros plus postage
surcharge where applicable.
Subscriptions: www.ancient-warfare.com
or Ancient Warfare PO Box 4082, 7200 BB Zutphen,
The Netherlands.

Distribution
Ancient Warfare is sold through selected retailers,
museums, the internet and by subscription.
If you wish to become a sales outlet, please contact the
editorial office or e-mail us: sales@ancient-warfare.com

Ancient Warfare is published every two months by
Karwansaray BV, Rotterdam, The Netherlands.
PO Box 1110, 3000 BC Rotterdam, The Netherlands.

ISSN: 1874-7019
ISBN: 978-94-90258-00-9

Printed in the European Union

CONTENTS

4 PRESENTING MARATHON THEN AND NOW
Evaluating the importance of the battle

7 THE ROAD TO WAR
Greco-Persian relations before the Ionian revolt

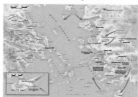

12 GETTING A BALANCED VIEW
Sources for the battle of Marathon and the Persian Wars

18 REVOLTS IN IONIA
The first major conflicts, 500/499-494/493

23 PRELUDE TO MARATHON
The battle of Ephesus - 498 BC

30 MARATHON DAWN
The Persians cross the Aegean

34 HOW DID THE BATTLE OF MARATHON GO DOWN?
Comparing recent reconstructions

44 THE BLINDING OF EPIZELUS
Battlefield stress in ancient Greek warfare

49 MEANWHILE, IN SPARTA
Why were the Spartans late for Marathon?

53 THE RISE AND FALL OF ATHENS AND PERSIA
The aftermath of Marathon

60 STORM OF SPEARS AND PRESS OF SHIELDS
The mechanics of hoplite battle

69 A CRAZE FOR SCALES
Dress and equipment of the Greek forces

77 THE ARMY OF ALL NATIONS
The Achaemenid army at Marathon

86 THE ENEMY THROUGH GREEK EYES
Dress and equipment on the Persian side

94 REMEMBERING MARATHON
War and public monuments in ancient Greece

98 AT THE TOMB OF MARATHON AND BEYOND
Tips for visiting the area

Evaluating the importance of the battle

Presenting Marathon then and now

It is often said that Marathon was one of the few really decisive battles in history. The truth, however, is that we cannot establish this with certainty. Still, the fight had important consequences: it gave rise to the idea that East and West were opposites, an idea that has survived until the present day, in spite of the fact that 'Marathon' has become the standard example to prove that historians should really refrain from such bold statements.

By Jona Lendering

The Spartans were the first to commemorate the battle of Marathon. Although they arrived too late for the fight, they visited the battlefield, inspected the dead, and praised the Athenians. The story is told by Herodotus (*Histories* 6.120), the author of our main source for the fight, and the very first question we should ask is why he decided to tell it. After all, his ambition was to record "great and marvelous deeds", and the late arrival of the reinforcements was neither great nor marvelous. The Spartan presence at Marathon, however, enabled Herodotus to present a battle as a fight that mattered to all Greeks.

'Marathon' was more than just a normal battle between Athenians and Persians: this idea was hardly new. As Natascha Sojc shows in her article (page 94) monuments had already been erected, prior to Herodotus' writing, which presented the warriors as the equals of the heroes of the Trojan War. Other monuments, like the one mentioned by Pausanias, presented the dead as defenders of democracy: He mentions an Athenian "grave in the plain with stones on it, carved with the names of the dead in their voting districts" (*Guide for Greece* 1.32.3). The monument erected in Delphi presented the ten tribes and lauded the democratically elected

Miltiades, but conspicuously ignored the polemarch Callimachus (see Peter Krentz's article on p.34 and further for a debate about his importance).

Framing the battle

Herodotus chose to present the fight as a panhellenic battle. Knowing that the Persians had returned in 480 and had tried to conquer Greece, he interpreted Marathon as a first attempt to do the same, which made the fight important for all of Greece. This is unlikely to be a correct judgment: the Persian army was too small for conquest and occupation, and most historians have rejected Herodotus' spin on events.

What they did not reject was the context in which Herodotus presented the violent actions. His *Histories* presuppose an elaborate model of action and reaction, which is Herodotus' way to express historical causality: Cyrus conquered the Greek towns in Asia (action), they revolted (reaction), a war broke out in which Athens and Eretria supported the rebels (action), Persia restored order and decided to subdue the allies (reaction), the Persians came to Attica (action), where the Athenians defeated them at Marathon (reaction), so the Persians returned with a bigger army to avenge themselves.

This pattern of action and reaction is unlikely to correspond to the historical facts. After all, the first action and the first reaction are separated by a considerable period, and the campaign of 490 was not aimed at the *conquest* of Greece. So, while Herodotus' *sequence* of the events between 500 and 479 is probably correct, we may have some doubt about the *causal connections*. The man from Halicarnassus may in the end turn out to be right, but that is not now at issue: what needs to be stressed is that Herodotus created the framework in which we place the battle of Marathon.

This framework also presents the struggle between the Greeks and the Asians as going back to times immemorial. The very first part of *The Histories* is a slightly ironic account of some ancient legends about women being carried away, but Herodotus continues by pointing at "the man who to the best of my knowledge was the first to commit wrong against the Greeks", king Croesus of Lydia. The restriction "to the best of my knowledge" suggests that Herodotus believed that the conflict had started earlier. Herodotus is not just the father of history, he is also the father of the idea that East and West are eternal opposites.

Even more importantly, he is the first author to make this antagonism something more than a geographical opposition. In his eyes, the Asians were the slaves of the Great King, who went to war because the ruler ordered them to, while the Greeks were citizens of free cities, who obeyed the law and went to defend their liberty. This is borne out by the words of the Spartan exile Demaratus to Xerxes: "Over the Greeks is set Law as a master, whom they fear much more even than your people fear you" (7.103). This speech is, of course, one of Herodotus' own compositions: not only are 'tragic warners' in

The Histories invariably speaking on behalf of the author, but the topic under discussion, the tension between the rule of a leader and the rule of the law, is typical for the political debate in democratic Athens (compare the famous, equally fictitious constitutional debate in 3.80-82).

Herodotus' framing of the Persian Wars as a struggle between a monarchical Asia and a free Greece explains his authorial choices. He might have mentioned the Spartan visit to the battlefield very briefly, but inserted a long digression, because the incident, although irrelevant for the battle, was useful to convert Marathon into a panhellenic event.

Nineteenth-century theories

Greece versus Asia: although popular in the classical age, this theme lost relevance in the Hellenistic age. Once Rome had seized power, the main opposition was that between the barbarians outside the Empire and the civilized Mediterranean city dwellers. When Christianity became popular, the main antagonism was that between pagans and orthodox believers.

In the Early Middle Ages, new self-identifications and oppositions arose: the scholars of Constantinople believed that Islam was the archenemy of the Byzantine Empire, and in the West, people believed in an antagonism between Islam and those who were called 'Europenses'. The first reference to Europeans as a cultural unity is the *Mozarabic Chronicle of 754*.

For centuries, the inhabitants of western Europe associated their culture with Rome and Christianity. In the eighteenth century, however, the famous German art historian Johann Joachim Winckelmann created the modern paradigm that Rome had merely continued Greek culture, and that Athens was the real origin of western civilization. This new idea was successful, and in the early nineteenth century, the belief that Athens was the cradle of a freedom-loving, rational European civilization, was fully accepted. It was freedom, philosophers argued, that had been defended by the Athenians at Marathon. Because their victory had inspired other Greeks to resist Xerxes, Marathon had been an important battle: in Marathon, the foundations of

western civilization had been laid. The British philosopher John Stuart Mill judged that "the battle of Marathon, even as an event in English history, is more important than the battle of Hastings."

That bold, often repeated statement, is based on three assumptions. The first is that the Athenians were fighting for the independence of Greece. The pre-Herodotean monuments prove that this was not the perspective of the participants: Athenian democrats fighting against a Persian army that wanted to bring back the tyrant Hippias. As indicated above, it was Herodotus who stressed the willingness of Sparta to go to war as well, and introduced the panhellenic element.

The second assumption is that the *political* independence of Greece guaranteed the freedom of its *culture*. In 1901, the great German historian Eduard Meyer wrote in his *Geschichte des Altertums* ("History of Antiquity") that the consequences of a Persian victory in 490 or 480 would have been serious.

Three fragments of the inscriptions on the monument Pausanias mentions were recently excavated in Astros on the Peloponnese, where the Athenian billionaire Herodes Atticus (second century AD) owned a villa. He apparently removed the inscriptions from the monument seen by Pausanias. The names were indeed arranged by voting districts, which means that the original tomb was a monument of the Athenian democracy. Greek archaeologist G. Spyropoulos has suggested that the famous funeral mound in the plain was erected at the same time. This would explain why the dead were buried in a tumulus: a very aristocratic type of burial that had come to an end after the reforms of Solon (594 BC), had no parallels in classical Athens, cannot have been used in 490, but may well have been deemed suitable in the Roman age, when the aristocratic associations were no longer remembered.
The soros *on the plain of Marathon, the burial mound for the Athenian fallen.*

© Livius.org

Eduard Meyer (1855-1930)

Max Weber (1864-1920)

"The end result would have been that some kind of religion [...] would have put Greek thought under a yoke, and any free spiritual life would have been bound in chains. The new Greek culture would, just like oriental culture, have been of a theocratic-religious nature."

The argument is, more or less, that the Great King would have replaced democracy with tyranny, so that the free Athenian civilization would have vanished in a maelstrom of oriental despotism, irrationality, and cruelty. Without democracy, no Greek philosophy, no innovative Greek literature, no arts, no rationalism. In this sense, the Greek victory in the Persian Wars was decisive for Greek culture.

The third assumption is that there is continuity from ancient Greece to nineteenth-century Europe. This sociological statement has never been properly tested, even though there is an obvious counterargument: after the fall of Rome, people did not recognize this continuity. As we saw the 'Europeans' were not recognized as a cultural unity until 754, and when they were, they were Frankish Christians fighting Iberian Muslims, not Greeks fighting Asians. Some scholars (e.g. Anthony Pagden) have tried to solve this problem by arguing that, in spite of the fact that nobody had noticed it, the spirit of freedom had always been there, just like the spirit of monarchism had always remained alive in the East, influencing individual behavior. This type of argument is called 'ontological holism', and is better known from Marx' notorious idea that history was forged by the struggle between classes, or the equally notorious idea that history was a war between races. Class struggle, race war, or the clash between free Europe and tyrannical Asia are abstractions that do not really exist.

A more sophisticated way to refute the counterargument is the idea, best known from Jacob Burckhardt's famous *Civilization of the Renaissance in Italy* (1860), is that the Renaissance was a rebirth of Roman civilization and that Winckelmann was the first scholar who understood that Roman civilization had been a continuation of Athenian civilization. This cannot be discarded out of hand, because social scientists have never developed the tools to test such bold statements about continuity.

Meyer's view assessed

Today, the German scholar Max Weber is best known as the father of sociology, but he started his career as an ancient historian. In 1904/1905, he published two 'Critical Studies in the Logic of Cultural Sciences', in which he investigated the nature and scope of the limits of our study of the past. The second essay deals with 'Objective Possibility and Adequate Causation in Historical Explanation', and has become rightly famous. As it happens, one of Weber's examples is Meyer's analysis of the meaning of Marathon, which is shown to be the result of a counterfactual argument: if the Persians had won, the preconditions would not have been met for the rise of Athenian civilization. But, Weber argued, this was nothing but speculation. Counterfactual arguments are usually fallacious.

For example, how did Meyer know that the Persians, after a victory in the Persian Wars, would have put an end to democracy? We must pause for thought when we read that Herodotus explicitly states that the Persian commander Mardonius supported Greek democracy (*Histories* 6.43). Another point is that very few historians, right now, will accept that the ancient Near East was 'of a theocratic-religious nature': it was in Persian Babylonia that astronomers developed the scientific method. Plato and Aristotle might have lived in a Persian Athens. Likewise, Eric Dodds' *The Greeks and the Irrational* (1951) meant the end of the idea that Greek culture represented a more rational view of life.

So, Meyer's reading of the Persian War has been decisively challenged. We cannot make bold statements about the meaning of Marathon. Unfortunately, not everybody is aware that there are limits to what we can understand about the past: over the past years, several books have appeared that pretend that there is a direct continuity from Marathon to our own age. Historians and social scientists really have something important to discuss. ●

Jona Lendering is the webmaster of Livius.Org and is a regular contributor to Ancient Warfare.

Further reading
Weber's critical studies are better known to continental European than Anglo-Saxon historians. They have been translated into English, however, and can be found in Max Weber, *The methodology of the Social Sciences* (1949). A PDF can be downloaded at http://tinyurl.com/3q2jcbg.

Greco-Persian relations before the Ionian Revolt

The road to war

When historians talk about watersheds, pivotal points, events that changed the course of history, sooner or later the discussion almost inevitably turns to the Greco-Persian Wars. For some, the battle of Marathon is a more decisive event than the battles of Salamis and Plataea. Some even go further. To quote John Stuart Mill: "The battle of Marathon, even as an event in British history, is more important than the battle of Hastings."

By Seán Hußmann

An Athenian drinking cup moulded as the face of a fearful Persian. Having emerged victorious from the Persian wars, Athenians were full of confidence and eager to remind themselves of their successes. Now in the British Museum, London.

© Karwansaray Publishers

Positions like Mill's can be (and indeed have been) questioned. Still, Marathon certainly was one of the more important battles of the Greco-Persian wars, a series of conflicts that began with the Ionian revolt in 500/499 BC and, it can be argued, was only resolved when Alexander the Great conquered the Persian Empire.

However, pivotal battles and turning-points of history do not just happen; they usually are a part of greater, underlying historical processes. Similarly, the Greco-Persian conflict did not materialize out of thin air. The Ionian Revolt did not happen in isolation. Let us therefore examine the historical and mythological roots of this conflict.

Faultlines of conflict

Greek settlement of the Aegean islands and coastal areas goes back at least into the late second millennium BC. Miletus for example, a city that had been populated since the fourth millennium BC and was destroyed around 1100 BC, was – according to legend – resettled by Ionian Greek colonists in 1053 BC. The phases of Hellenic expansion throughout the Mediterranean, the 'Ionian Colonization' during the 11th and 10th century BC and the 'Great Colonization' from the 8th to the 6th century BC, served to strengthen the ties between the Greek mainland in Europe and the poleis in Asia Minor. The Aegean, its coastlines and islands had in effect become a Greek sea.

Greek city-states valued their political autonomy; indeed, their passionate defense of this autonomy was an important part of Greek polis-culture. So even if Greek settlements around the Aegean were a politically divided conglomeration of independent – and often antagonistic – city-states, it was nevertheless this political fragmentation that was the basis for Greek political culture and identity. Culturally the Greeks saw the Aegean Sea as a unity, the Greek *Oikumene*.

If we are to believe Herodotus, the conflict between Greeks and barbarians (by no means being a pejorative term here, but rather a Greek expression for anyone who does not speak Greek; Herodotus, of course, uses it mainly for Persians) goes at least as far back into mythological times as the Greek settlement of Ionia does. In his version, it was the Phoenicians, not Zeus himself, who kidnapped Io while they were trading with the Greeks in Argos – a blatant insult to Greek *proxenia* ("hospitality"). The Greeks however got their revenge by abducting Europa, the daughter of the king of Tyre. After thus having repaid the Phoenicians in their own currency, Herodotus tells us, some Greeks overstepped the line and committed the second serious offence (the first having been committed by the Phoenicians in stealing away Io) in Greco-Barbarian relations. They abducted Medea, the daughter of the king of Colchis.

"And the king of Colchis sent a herald to the land of Hellas and demanded satisfaction for the rape and to have his daughter back; but they answered that, as the Barbarians had given them no satisfaction for the rape of Io the Argive, so neither would they give satisfaction to the Barbarians for this."

Herodotus, Histories 1.2

Disregarding this interesting justification the Greeks gave the king of Colchis for their behavior, they certainly set a bad example for following generations of mythological figures on both sides. Inspired by the practice of stealing women and enticed by the fact that "he would not be compelled to give any satisfaction for this wrong" (Herodotus 1.3), Paris, son of Priam and prince of Troy, stole Helen from her husband Menelaos, king of Sparta, disregarding the sacred rules of *proxenia* – just as the Phoenicians had done when stealing Io. Compelled by the oath that Odysseus had had the Greek kings swear, to honor Helen's and Menelaos' marriage, they went to war over this crime. For this, as Herodotus puts it,

"the Hellenes were very greatly to blame; for they set the first exam-

ple of war, making an expedition into Asia before the Barbarians made any into Europe. [...] And the Persians say that they, namely the people of Asia, when their women were carried away by force, had made it a matter of no account, but the Hellenes on account of a woman [...] destroyed the dominion of Priam; and that from this time forward they had always considered the Hellenic race to be their enemy: for Asia and the Barbarian races which dwell there the Persians claim as belonging to them."

Herodotus, Histories 1.4

From mythology to history

Herodotus explicitly mentions the Persian universal claim to power in Asia. This claim naturally stood in conflict with the Greek *poleis*, their propensity to political autonomy and their perception of the Aegean Sea as integral part of the Greek *Oikumene*. However, in Herodotus' history, it was not the Persians who first subjected Greek poleis in Asia Minor to foreign rule, but rather the Lydian king, Croesus, whose name has become synonymous with unimaginable wealth.

The Lydians did not interfere with the inner autonomy of their Greek subjects – most pre-Roman empires in antiquity were content with having their subjects pay a more or less regular tribute and provide soldiers for their imperial masters' military campaigns. King Croesus even made rich offerings and donations to Greek poleis and temples, particularly to the temple of Apollo in Delphi, and we know that the Lydian elite developed a taste for Greek culture and embraced Greek lifestyle. It did not take long for the Lydian upper class to become Hellenized (as opposed to Medized – becoming Persian). Still, having to pay tribute in money and men was a large enough encroachment on the autonomy of the Greek poleis for them to harbor resentments against the Lydians.

At the height of its power, the Lydian empire stretched from the Aegean coast in the west to the river Halys in the east. Power, greed and – ultimately – *hybris*

(pride or arrogance) are topics that Herodotus loves to explore in his work. So it comes as no surprise to his readers to learn that Croesus was not content with ruling the sizeable portion of Asia Minor that was already his. Croesus wanted more, and more was to be had in the east, beyond the Halys.

A fateful oracle

In archaic times Greece saw the rise of the *polis* and its citizen-soldier, the heavy infantryman so characteristic for the Greek culture of war, the hoplite, who fought side by side with his fellow citizens in the phalanx. At the same time the East, from the coast of Asia Minor to the Indus river, saw a succession of rising and falling empires. To simplify this history, suffice to say that the Persian Dynasty of the Achaemenids finally arose as the dominant power in this region. The Persians, originally a pastoral, nomadic people that had migrated from the central Asian steppes to roughly modern-day Iran, had overthrown their former masters, the Medes, thus forming the nucleus of what was later to become the Persian empire. Ruled by Cyrus the Great, this young, dynamic empire rapidly expanded its rule until it too, bordered the river Halys.

For Croesus, expanding his borders consequently meant war with Persia. However Herodotus portrays him, Croesus was no fool. He knew that he needed help in overthrowing this new, mighty empire. Since there was no help to be had in the east, he turned to the west – to the Greeks. The Greek poleis under his rule naturally had to supply him with funds and soldiers, but Croesus went further. He formed an alliance with the largest military power in Greece – Sparta. Being supported by Greek spears, however, still wouldn't be enough to take on the Persians. So Croesus took the next logical step and sought the assistance of Greek gods. Croesus had already courted the Delphic Apollo and lavished royal gifts on his temples; now, he expected a favorable oracle from the god.

As anyone who has ever studied ancient history knows, the Delphic Oracle was famously ambivalent and its oracles wildly open to interpretation. "If you cross the Halys, you will destroy a great empire", was what Apollo told Croesus through the priestess Pythia. Encouraged by this oracle, Croesus indeed crossed the Halys and invaded Cappadocia, the region just east of the border, after the conquest of Urartu in 547. He captured the city of Pteria and its neighboring cities and sold their inhabitants into slavery to cover part of the costs of his military adventure. His first open confrontation with Cyrus' army took place outside Pteria. The initial battle was bloody and casualty rates on both sides were high, but brought no clear result: Herodotus records it as a stalemate. The day after the battle, Croesus offered battle again, but Cyrus did not accept. As the campaigning season was nearing its end, Croesus therefore marched back home to Lydia and, expecting no more military action that year, disbanded large parts of his army. There is, after all, no sense in paying mercenaries when they are not needed.

This, however, proved to have been a serious miscalculation on Croesus' part, for Cyrus was by no means resigned to postpone the war's continuation until the next campaigning season. Instead, he pursued Croesus' largely diminished army and inflicted a devastating defeat on Croesus at Thymbra, on the plains to north of the Lydian capital, Sardis. According to Herodotus, it was Cyrus' camelry that won the day, their scent terrifying the Lydian cavalry's horses. Croesus was forced to retreat to Sardis, where he was besieged by the Persian army. After fourteen days of siege, the supposedly impregnable walls of Sardis were taken by the Persians and – just as the oracle had prophesized – a great empire was destroyed.

Cyrus meanwhile had sent envoys to the Greek poleis in Asia Minor demanding their surrender – a demand that was refused by every single Greek city except Miletus, the Greeks probably still trusting a favorable interpretation of Apollo's oracle. It was not until after the fall of Sardis that the Ionians showed themselves open to negotiations. Unfortunately for them, the time for negotiations and peaceful surrender was long gone. Cyrus himself went back east to conquer the Neo-Babylonian Empire and left his general, Harpagos, in Asia Minor to deal with the troublesome Greeks.

"The other Ionians except the Milesians did indeed contend in arms with Harpagos [...] fighting each for his own native city; but when they were defeated and captured they remained all in their own place and performed that which was laid upon them: but the Milesians [...] had made a sworn agreement with Cyrus himself and kept still. Thus for the second time Ionia had been reduced to subjection. And when Harpagos had conquered the Ionians on the mainland, then the Ionians who dwelt in the islands [...] gave themselves over to Cyrus."

Herodotus, Histories 1.169

Persian rule
After its conquest by the Persians, Lydia was transformed into a Persian *satrapy*, a province ruled by a *satrap* who acted as local representative of Cyrus, the 'king of kings.' As they had previously had to do under Lydian rule, the Ionian Greeks now had to pay tribute and – if called upon – provide contingents of troops to the Persian army. However, their new masters showed little respect for the Greek *poleis'* inner autonomy. Persian rule was enforced by placing men of whom the satraps approved in a position of power over the Greek cities. Tyrants, the Greeks called these men. Backed by the might of the Persian Empire, these tyrants could easily dominate or even dissolve local political institutions. Political decisions regarding the citizens' daily life were no longer made by the assembly of citizens or the council, but by a despot not accountable to the law of the *polis*, but rather to the Persian satrap. However mild and benevolent Persian rule turned out to be, in the eyes of a citizen proud of his *polis*, this went contrary to everything that he deemed politically right and just.

For the Ionian *poleis'* economy, Persian rule turned out to be a double-edged sword. On the one hand, the imperial peace and stability the Persians brought meant security for the overland trade-route into central Asia Minor and further into Mesopotamia. On the other hand, Persian conquests in the Levant had freed the Phoenicians from their former rulers. The Phoenicians, like the Greeks a seafaring and trading people, soon made their influence felt in the Mediterranean and became economic rivals of the Ionian traders.

As in the Levant, Persian expansion in other regions became an economic problem for the Ionian Greeks, too. Cyrus' successor, Cambyses II conquered Egypt in 525 BC. Archaeological evidence suggests that in the same year Naucratis, a Milesian colony in the Nile Delta, began to lose its significance as a Greek trading centre. Persian expeditions into Thrace and Scythia brought the Dardanelles under Persian control as well. This meant that Persia now controlled the trade-routes between the Mediterranean and the Black Sea. As many Greek cities were dependent on the import of grain from the Black Sea regions, the Persians thus gained a stranglehold on their Ionian subjects, not to mention tolls and tariffs on Ionian trade with the north. In effect, Persian expansion brought severe limitations on Greek trade in the eastern Mediterranean.

The economic decline of commercial hubs like Miletus was further hastened by the destruction of Sybaris, a Greek colony on the Gulf of Taranto in Italy and the Ionians' most important trading partner in the west.

Road to war
Having thus lost the last remnants of political autonomy and their previously prominent position as economic power, it comes as no surprise that the Ionian Greeks were less than satisfied with Persian rule. To put it more bluntly: Persian political and economic encroachment on the Greek *poleis* in Asia Minor had turned Ionia into a powder keg. It would not take more than a spark to entice the whole area to open revolt against Persia and to set events in motion that would ultimately lead to Greeks facing Persians in battle on the plain of Marathon. ●

Seán Hußmann is currently working on his PhD and is a lecturer of ancient history at the University Bonn.

Further reading:
- A.R. Burn, *Persia and the Greeks*. London 1962.
- M. Dandamaev, *A political history of the Achaemenid empire*. Leiden 1989.
- W. Will, *Die Perserkriege*. Munich 2010.

Main map labels:

25 50 75 100
KILOMETERS

Halonnesos

LARISSA
Meliboea?
Casthanaea?
Peneus
PELASGIOTIS
MAGNESIA
Crannon
THESSALIA
Scotussa
Bœbeis Lacus
Pherae
PHTHIOTIS
Pharsalus
Pagasae
Thebae P.
ACHAEA
PHTHIOTIS
Pagasaeus
Sinus
Sepias Promontorium
Mare Aegaeu
Heraclea
Othrys M.
1.726
Artemisium Promontorium
Peparethus
Achalan M.
Espercheus
Lammia
Scyros
AINIS
MALIS
Histiaea
Sinus Maliacus
Heraclea
Telethrius M.
Oeta M.
Thermopylae
Corax M.
DORIS
L. EPICNEMIDIA
Sinus Euboicus
DIAKRIA?
EUBOIA
Dirphys M.
ABANTES
Elateia
Opus
LOCRIS OPUNTIA
PHOCIS
Orchomenus
MESOCHOROS
Amphissa
Parnassus M.
Chaeronea
Copae
Euboia
Delphi
Lebadea
Copais L.
CHALCIS
LOCRIS
OZOLIS
Anticyra
BOEOTIA
Eretria
Aegium
Coronea
Helicon
Mons
THEBAE
Haliartus
Asopus
DRYOPES
Sinus Corinthiacus
Thespiae
Plateae
Cithaeron M.
1.016
Parnes M.
Diacria
Marathon 490
Ocha M.
MEGARIS
MEGARA
Pedias
Pentelicon
Carystus
CORINTHUS
Salamis
ATHENAE
Andros
ARCADIA
Phaleron
Andros
Caphyae
ATTICA
Keos
Orchomenus
Aegina
Sinus
Mantinea
Saronicus
Paralia
Tenos
ARGOS
Epidaurus
ARGOLIS
Tenos
Tegea
Sunium Promontorium
KYNOURIA
Troezen
Sinus Argolicus
Delos
SKIRTIS
Eurotas
Parnon M.
Delos
BELMINATIS
AIGYTIS
Taygetos
SPARTA
CYCLADES
Amyclae
Paros
Paros

Inset map (Cyprus):

0 25 50 75 100
KILOMETERS

Cilicius
Aulon
Crommyon Promontorium
Persian land force invasion 497 497
Plains of Salamis 496
Salamis
Acamas Promontorium
CYPRUS
Soloi
Melos
Kition
Melos
Trogodus Mons
Pedalium Promontorium
Kourion
Ionian combined fleet victory over Phoenicians 496
Paphos
Amathous
Approach of Phoenician fleet

C

Sources for the Battle of Marathon and the Persian Wars

Getting a balanced view

There can be no doubt whatsoever that Herodotus of Halicarnassus is the main reason for the fame of the Battle of Marathon and by far our most important source. His account is not without its problems however, and he has recently come in for substantial criticism. Fortunately, we do not have to depend on his writings alone. Both sides in this conflict have left corroborating evidence of various kinds.

By Allison Kirk and Michael J. Taylor

© Livius.org

"The Tribe of Erechtheus:
Fame, arriving eternally to
Gaia's gleaming frontier
Shall attest the excellence of
these men
That they fell fighting the Mede,
and so crowned Athens. As a few
withstood the war waged by so many

Drakontides, Antiphon, Aphsephes,
Chsenon, Glaukiades, Timochsenos,
Theognis, Diodoros, Euchsias,
Euphroniades, Euktemon, Kallias,
Antias, Tolmis, Thochudides, Dios,
Amunomachos, Leptines, Aischraios,
Peron, Phaodrias...".

SEG, 56.430, author's translation

Bust of Herodotus of Halicarnassus, alternatively praised as the 'Father of History' and torn down as a great 'liar', he is by far the most important source for the Greco-Persian wars and early Greek history in general. Now in the Agora Museum, Athens.

A Marathon casualty listing

This exciting new inscription, freshly published in the *Supplementum Epigraphicum Graecum* (SEG), and still subject to considerable controversy concerning the reconstruction and translation of the first line of the hexameter, contains a casualty listing for the Athenian Tribe of Erechtheus. While the inscription does not say explicitly that these men were killed in Marathon, the circumstantial evidence is overwhelming. The stone stele matches a description of the 2nd Century AD traveler Pausanias, who visited Marathon and saw the complete memorial (Pausanias 1.32.3). The object was found on the Peloponnesian estate of the Roman senator Herodes Atticus, who claimed descent from the Athenian general Miltiades, and thus would have had personal motives to loot the memorial in order to fill his home with Marathon related memorabilia. The numbers also add up. Assuming casualties were generally spread evenly between all ten Cleisthenic tribes, the twenty-two dead for Tribe of Erechtheus (although a few additional fragments may push that number to as high as twenty-nine) corresponds well to Herodotus' report of 192 total dead for the battle (Herodotus 6.117). Until now, we only knew the names of three of the fallen at Marathon, all elites: the *polemarch* ("War *Archon*") Callimachus, the *strategos* Stesilaus, and Cynegeirus, the brother of the playwright Aeschylus (Herodotus 6.114). This inscription and its list of honored dead is a reminder of the other citizens who fell fighting for their democracy.

Herodotus of Halicarnassus

Virtually everything we know about Marathon, the Persian Wars, and Greek history prior to 479 BC is rooted in the narrative work of Herodotus of Halicarnassus, who practically invented the modern genre of history. Herodotus was not simply trying to collect a narrow chronicle of deeds, or recount the tradition of a single community. Rather, he was engaged in investigative 'inquiry', in Ionian Greek *historiê*, from which our word 'history' is directly derived. Herodotus' title implied analysis, as he attempted to understand the cumulative impact of cause and effect upon the present situation. Herodotus wanted to know why the Greeks and Persians had engaged in warfare in the first place. Rather than seeking the answer in the recent past, he cast his net back across time and space, to the origins of both the mighty Persian Empire and the major Greek *poleis* that had confronted it.

Herodotus was born a subject of the Persian Empire in the Greek colony of Halicarnassus, now modern-day Turkey. His seems to have been exiled as a result of civic strife involving the Persian puppet tyrant of the city. The idea of conflict between Greek and Persian was therefore rooted in his own early experiences. He may have come of age on the island of Samos, but he subsequently moved to Athens, where he was a *metic*, a non-citizen foreigner. He was widely traveled, including to Egypt, and reportedly was a colonist in the Athenian settlement of Thurii, in southern Italy.

It is likely that Herodotus' completed his work in the early 420s BC. Our earliest allusions to his work comes from a play by Aristophanes datable to 425, while his references to contemporary events end in 429 BC with the murder of two Spartan envoys (7.137). Herodotus' history about the alliance of Athens and Sparta against the 'barbarian' must certainly be viewed in light of the Peloponnesian war then raging between those cities. While he spent time in Athens and admired the Athenian achievements at Marathon and Salamis, Herodotus offers a number of subtle critiques of Athenian imperialism: his history ends with the Athenians brutally lynching the Persian Artayktes, first stoning his son to death before his eyes (9.120).

Herodotus' method

Herodotus claims in his introduction that he is using the *grammateis* of both the Hellenes and Persians. What does he mean by this? He may have used the work of a number of pre-Socratic philosophers, men who like him traveled about asking questions and seeking answers. He was certainly inspired by poetic works of Homer and the Athenian tragedians. The image of the Spartans fighting over the body of Leonidas at Thermopylae (7.225), for example, is certainly indebted to the *Iliad*. Even if he often employs the irony of tragic plots in his various vignettes, it is notable that Herodotus' description of the Battle of Salamis differs substantially from that found in Aeschylus' *Persae*.

Herodotus may have been familiar with Persian historical inscriptions. His detailed knowledge about the ascension of Darius I suggests that he was familiar with the basic contents of the Behistun inscription (see below), which was known to circulate in manuscript form (a papyrus containing an Aramaic translation of the Behistun inscription was found at Elephantine). His record of Persian tribute lists (3.89-95) is likewise also probably derived from an official Persian listing, while he may use an official itinerary for his description of the Persian royal road (5.52-54).

Herodotus' most important sources, however, were oral. In some cases, he identifies vague oral traditions by noting that "they say that...." In other instances, Herodotus identifies particular sources. For the Battle of Marathon, he claims to have spoken with a veteran named Epizelus, who seems to have suffered from psychosomatic blindness as a result of battlefield trauma (6.117, see the article by Owen Rees in this issue).

Herodotus' reputation

Herodotus' reputation rises and falls with scholarly trends. The budding science of anthropology embraced Herodotus as the father of anthropology in the early 20th century, although by mid-century scholars fretted over his accuracy. In 1971, Detlev Fheling staked out 'the liar school' that peaked in the late 1980s. The tide turned again as post-modern scholars increasingly admired Herodotus for his cultural relativity and narratological bravado, bringing the cycle full circle.

Whatever the criticisms of Herodotus, if he is to be dismissed, then the project of Greek history prior to 480 BC must effectively be dismissed with him. While scholars generally agree on basic problems, and quibble about a large number of minor ones, his history is too important to be ignored. If Herodotus compares poorly to future Greek historians like Thucydides and Polybius, he without question is superior to any of his competition on the Persian Wars (see below). Other writers provide information that only fleshes out the narrative of Herodotus, and indeed, where there are conflicts, Herodotus is generally to be preferred. While imperfect, Herodotus deserves his title as "Father of History" (*pater historiae*, Cicero, *De Legibus* 1.5). If Thucydides and Polybius were better objective historians, it is largely because they benefited from Herodotus' groundbreaking example, and were able to learn from his mistakes.

The lost history of Ctesias of Cnidos

Ctesias of Cnidos, a Greek who served as the personal physician to the Persian King Artaxerxes II (r.404-358 BC), composed a history which challenged Herodotus' version of events. Unfortunately, Ctesias' full text has been lost. It survives in several fragments, mostly from a summary provided by the Byzantine bishop Photius (*Bibliotheca*, 72). Photius, who eventually served two tumultuous tours as Patriarch of Constantinople, spent time in Baghdad on an embassy in the 840s AD, and may have stumbled upon the works of Ctesias preserved by Arab librarians, who at this time were collecting obscure Greek texts which were becoming extinct in both Byzantium and the Medieval West.

While Ctesias should have enjoyed access to Persian court archives and oral traditions, what little we have of his history does not inspire confidence. The narrative of Marathon, as summarized by Photius, is truncated. The only major difference from Herodotus is that Ctesias claims that Datis, the Persian commander was killed in the battle, and that the Athenians refused to return his body. According to Ctesias, the failure to return the body was a major justification for Xerxes' subsequent invasion. Herodotus has Datis return home safely (6.119).

However, Ctesias' history of the second Persian invasion suffers poorly in comparison to Herodotus. Ctesias mentions the stand of Leonidas at Thermophylae, but then places the 300 Spartans under the command of Pausanias at Plataea! Ctesias seems to have badly confused his chronology, as he puts the land battle at Plataea before the naval battle at Salamis, and lists the Spartan troop strength at Thermopylae as their numbers at Plataea. Writing explicitly to challenge Herodotus, Ctesias may have filled his history with details designed to contradict his rival, rather than to reflect researched historical facts. The fragments of Ctesias mostly make us appreciate that Herodotus has survived in full.

Later biographies

We have an alternative vision of the Battle of Marathon in the short biography of the Athenian general Miltiades, written by the late-Republican biographer Cornelius Nepos (fl. 50 BC). Nepos does provide us with a key point of information that Herodotus neglects: the Athenian troop

Rare inscriptions provide the only near-contemporary sources for the conflict. Apart from the memorial at Marathon, fragmented epigrams possibly by the poet Simonides survive memorializing the heroic defenders of the Athenian polis. To which battle the epigrams belong is, unsurprisingly, fiercely debated.

strength of 9000 Athenian hoplites and 1000 Plateans. This figure is surely plausible, and is in keeping with other evidence for Athenian mobilization, including the 8000 Athenian hoplites at Plataea in 479 (Herodotus. 9.28). Nepos' report of 100,000 Persian infantry and 10,000 cavalry should be dismissed. Nepos' tactical overview of the battle is in stark contrast to Herodotus. Whereas Herodotus has the Athenians attack the Persians at a run, Nepos claims that it is Datis who foolishly attacks the Greek defensive positions, only to suffer defeat. It is unclear what Nepos' source for this is, but he seldom excels as a military historian. Given the choice between Herodotus and Nepos, Herodotus wins hands down.

Plutarch, a Boeotian writing c. 100 AD, had little love for Herodotus and his canonical status. Amongst his writing is a scathing attack entitled *On the Malice of Herodotus*. Plutarch in part reiterates criticisms of Herodotus that go back to Thucydides and Aristotle: that he gets facts mixed up, that he accepts charming stories as reality, etc. But Plutarch, a local Greek patriot who idealized the bygone era of Greek's golden age, was resentful of Herodotus' dubious depiction of his beloved Boeotia (and especially the Medizing city of Thebes), and the fawning attentions devoted to Athens and Sparta. Plutarch, who wanted his classical

heroes in soft focus, ultimately criticized Herodotus for being too realistic, daring to discuss Greek communities who went over to the Persians along with heroes like Miltiades and Pausanius who were all too tragically human.

Plutarch himself provides us with a short account of the Battle of Marathon in his *Life of Aristides*. Whereas Herodotus has the Athenian center break completely, Plutarch has it tenuously held by Aristides and Themistocles.

A Persian view?

Dio Cocceianus Chrysostom ("the Gold-tongue", fl. 100 AD) was rhetor active during the so-called 'Second Sophistic', a renaissance based upon the art of public declamation. Chrysostom was a Greek patriot whose academic interests hearkened back to the glory days of Classical Greece, even as he lived a comfortable life as a Roman citizen. Widely read, he includes in his eleventh oration what may be a fragment from an official Persian history of the Greco-Persian wars:

"*I heard, for instance, a Mede declare that the Persians concede none of the claims made by the Greeks, but maintain that Darius dispatched Datis and Artaphernes against Naxos and Eretria, and*

that after capturing these cities they returned to the king; that, however, while they were lying at anchor off Euboea, a few of their ships were driven on to the Attic coast — not more than twenty — and their crews had some kind of an engagement with the inhabitants of that place; that, later on, Xerxes in his expedition against Greece conquered the Lacedaemonians at Thermopylae and slew their king Leonidas, then captured and razed the city of the Athenians and sold into slavery all who did not escape; and that after these successes he laid tribute upon the Greeks and withdrew to Asia. Now it is quite clear that this is a false account, but, since it was the natural thing to do, it is quite possible that the king ordered this story to be spread among the upland tribes in order to keep them quiet."

Dio Cocceianus Chrysostom 11.148-149 (Loeb translation)

Unfortunately, we cannot know for sure whether this passage reflects a fragment from an 'official' history or simply Dio's sophistic imagining of what such an official history might have looked like. For the

Marathon invasion, the Persians could in all honesty claim that they had achieved substantial accomplishments in the capture of the island of Naxos and the sack of Eretria; Marathon could be dismissed as a minor skirmish. Indeed, a tapestry in Babylon, reported by the dubious source Philostratus, supposedly also depicted victories at Naxos and Eretria, while neglecting Marathon (*Life of Apollonius* 1.25). According to Dio, the second Persian war required more obfuscation, correctly celebrating the annihilation of Leonidas, the sack of Athens and the submission of many Greek communities, but consigning to oblivion the serious defeats at Salamis and Plataea.

Administrative records
One of the great frustrations of writing about the Persian Wars is the fact that the narrative sources, discussed above, are exclusively Greek. The Persians were the master of the most sophisticated empire the world had seen, capable of mustering vast material resources and military manpower, while negotiating the cultural politics of ruling a decentralized array of tribal groupings and formerly independent kingdoms. While we may not have their narrative viewpoint for the Persian War, Persian sources can tell us much about the Persian imperial system which confronted the nucleated Greek *poleis*.

The University of Chicago's excavations at Persepolis in the 1930s unearthed two of the richest Persian sources for the period of the Greco-Persian wars: The Persepolis Fortification Archive and the Persepolis Treasury Archive, both named

according to their findspots. Darius I founded Persepolis, near modern Shiraz (Iran), as one of the capitals of the Achaemenid Persian Empire. These archives are such vital sources because they both have clear archaeological contexts and clear temporal ranges which situate them in the heartland capital of the Achaemenid empire during the reign of the ruler who dispatched troops to Marathon.

The tablets that make up the Persepolis Fortification Archive represent the administrative records of a food procurement and ration system. The texts from the archive deal with the procurement of commodities and the distribution of food rations to travelers on the royal road between Persepolis and Susa, workers (mainly agricultural), administrators, courtiers and the royal family in the various administrative regions of the system. There are some 20,000 - 30,000 clay artifacts in the archive and they span the time period between 509-494 BC. The archive contains three types of documents: tablets written in cuneiform Elamite, tablets written in Aramaic in ink, and uninscribed tablets. The tablets are very often sealed. Seals, very much like signet rings, are commonly used as authorization on important documents in the ancient Near East. During the Achaemenid empire, cylinder seals are most common; these are cylinders carved in the negative so that when they are rolled on wet clay the design emerges.

Fortification tablet Q1809 may provide a direct link between the Persepolis Fortification tablets and the Greco-Persian conflicts. The text provides royal authorization for travel provisions while returning from Sardis to one Datiya. This Datiya is generally believed to be the same Datis who would later lead the Persian expeditionary force at Marathon. Since the tablet dates to February-March 494 BC, it may refer to a reconnaissance mission undertaken during the Ionian revolt.

"Datiya received seven kegs of beer as rations. He carried a sealed document to the king. He left from Sardis via the royal post and went to the king at Persepolis. 11th Month, Year 27."

PFT Q-1809, translation following R.T. Hallock

The Persians do not often talk about the Greeks. When they do, Greeks are uniformly categorized as Ionians (*yauna*). Various tablets and inscriptions mention Ionians divided into four sub-categories: Ionians "of the land" referred to those who lived on the mainland of Asia Minor. Ionians "who are on the sea" described those Greeks who lived on the Aegean islands. The Ionians "beyond the sea" lumped together the various *poleis* of mainland Greece. The Ionians "in farmer's hats" described the Macedonians and their characteristic broad-brimmed hats. Thus while the Greeks tended to divide the world broadly into 'Hellenes' and 'barbarians' (*barbaroi*), the Persians, accustomed to both internal and external ethnic diversity, viewed the Greeks as a diverse and fragmented people. Equally interesting is the fact that while the Greeks did not consider the medizing Macedonians to be fully Greek, the Persians classified them as Ionians, albeit ones with funny hats.

The thousands of seal impressions preserved on the Persepolis Fortification and Treasury tablets are the closest thing that the Persian Empire had to a 'mainstream media.' The most frequent contact that an official or inhabitant of the Persian empire had with government sponsored visual propaganda was through seeing the imprints on clay documents. The most common image among these impressions is a royal hero (a figure wearing a crown and court robe) between two rampant animals subduing them with his bare hands. The second most common image is a

royal hero shooting an arrow at an animal attacking another animal. The image of the royal archer would be a reoccurring motif in Persian royal monuments, and was in keeping with the important military role archers played in the Persian army (e.g. Herodotus 7.218, 226).

Persian imperial monuments

Darius I was about sixty when he sent a modest fleet against Naxos, Eretria and Attica in 490 BC. We have two royal inscriptions that tell us how he wished himself to be portrayed to his subjects. While neither inscription pertains directly to the Battle of Marathon, both are important for understanding the imperial ideology of the Persian warrior kings. Whereas Aeschylus portrayed the ghost of Darius in his *Persae* as a somber and self-reflective figure, the man in charge of the Persian Empire in 490 BC was one characterized by deep religious piety and often brutal self-confidence.

The Behistun relief is cut into a cliff face abutting a major ancient road leading from Babylon to Ecbatana. In the main tableau, Darius stands with one foot on a prostrate enemy holding a bow in his left hand and making a gesture to Ahuramazda who hovers above and to the right in a winged disk. Behind Darius stands a bow bearer, and a spear bearer; each weapon bearer holds in their right hand their respective weapon. In front of Darius is a single file row of nine captives, the hands of each tied behind their backs, and all bound together by a rope around

their necks.

Behistun is the only extant victory monument from the entire Achaemenid period. The trilingual inscription that accompanies the relief recounts Darius I's overthrow of an 'illegitimate usurper' to become king. In opposition to the dynamic combat scenes on seal impressions from the Persepolis Archives, Darius I's relief at Behistun is a static royal symbol of victory and legitimate kingship. The composition is situated within a strong tradition of royal victory monuments in ancient Iraq and Iran, connecting Darius I to several legitimate and powerful kings. The bow is a Neo-Assyrian type, physically connecting Darius I's rule to the Neo-Assyrian empire - the largest empire the world had seen prior to the Persian empire. Darius uses familiar imagery in a different composition to make a statement about kingship.

Darius I's tomb at Naqsh-i Rustam is an innovative funerary monument as the first rock cut tomb with exterior relief decoration used as a royal tomb in Iran. The relief panel appears above an architectural facade, the door of which is the entrance to the tomb. In the central vignette, Darius I stands on a platform facing an altar on which there is a flame. Darius I holds the

A Persian Fortification cylinder seal (left) with its 'print' to the right, showing a Persian killing a very detailed Greek hoplite. Now in the Metropolitan Museum, New York.

© Livius.org

omitted), the second is a first person statement of the moral code by which Darius I lived and his capabilities as a warrior.

"Trained am I both with hands and with feet. As a horseman I am a good horseman. As a bowman I am a good bowman both afoot and on horseback. As a spearman I am a good spearman both afoot and on horseback."

DN 8h, translation by Roland G. Kent)

Here again the bow is the central symbol, in keeping with the quip by Herodotus that noble Persians learned to ride horses, shoot arrows and tell the truth (Herodotus 1.136).

Persian coinage

The image of the archer reoccurs also in another key medium of royal propaganda, coinage. Persian coins, however, generally neither circulated nor were produced in the heart of the Persian empire, but rather on its western-most fringes, given that coinage was central to exchange in the eastern Mediterranean, where the concept first arose. Therefore coins minted by a Persian king contained a stern message to his western subjects. The type I archer shows a bearded half-figure in profile wearing a dentate crown and Persian Court Robe. This figure holds a bow in his left hand, strings facing him, and two arrows in his right hand. The type II coin shows a bearded full-length figure wearing the Persian court robe and a dentate crown facing right in kneeling posture, indicative of a running motion. The figure is shown drawing an arrow on his bow and has a quiver full of arrows on his back. Both types are generally held to date to the reign of Darius I.

The isolated image of an archer in royal paraphernalia begs to be inserted into one of the numerous scenes of an archer killing an animal attacking another in the Persepolis Fortification Archive. The king is hunting predatory creatures and protecting weak flocks. The coins present a choice to the inhabitants of the western-

most regions of the Empire: you can be either the hunted or the protected. The Athenian merchant who donned armor to march to Marathon might very well have left behind a chest full of Persian archers, whose images were an unnerving reminder of the arrows he must face if he dared to stand in the way of Darius the Great. ●

Allison Kirk holds a M.A. in Ancient History and Mediterranean Archaeology from U.C. Berkeley. Michael J. Taylor is a regular contributor to Ancient Warfare.

Further reading
Examples of Persian inscriptions, the fragments of Ctesias, and an excellent introduction to Herodotus can be found at Jona Lendering's website www.livius.org.
- J.M. Bigwood, 'Ctesias as a Historian of the Persian Wars', in: *Phoenix* 32.1 (1978).
- C. Dewald and J. Marincola, *The Cambridge Companion to Herodotus*. Cambridge 2006.
- N. A. Doenges, 'The Campaign and Battle of Marathon', in: *Historia: Zeitshrift fur Alte Geschichte* 47.1 (1998).
- D. Fehling, *Herodotus and his "Sources:" Citation, Invention and the Narrative Art*. Leeds 1989.
- M. Garrison, 'Archers at Persepolis: The Emergence of Royal Ideology at the Heart of the Empire.', in J. Curtis and St. John Simpson (eds.), *The World of Achaemenid Persia, History, Art and Society in Iran and the Ancient Near East*. London 2010, pp. 337-68.
- A.W. Gomme, 'Herodotus and Marathon', in: *Phoenix* 6.3 (1952).
- W.K. Pritchett, *The Liar School of Herodotus*. Amsterdam 1993.
- M. Root, *The King and Kingship in Achaemenid Art: Essays on the Creation of an Iconography of Empire*. Acta Iranica Monograph Series, Vol. I9. Leiden l979.
- R. B. Strassler (ed.), *The Landmark Herodotus*. New York 2007.

© Karwansaray Publishers

'Died on the field of battle' - an Athenian casualty list for soldiers of the same tribe as mentioned above, now in the Louvre, Paris. These casualties fell during the middle of the fifth century. Maintaining the status and integrity of the Delian League required regular campaigns.

top end of the bow with his left hand. The bottom end of the bow rests on his foot. His right hand gestures to Ahuramazda who hovers above as a bust emerging from a winged disk and makes the same hand gesture as Darius I. This entire scene appears on top of a platform supported by two tiers of figures who represent the thirty lands of the empire. Two trilingual inscriptions accompany the relief. One is a first person account of Darius I's reign (the minor setback at Marathon naturally

The first major conflicts, 500/499-494/3
Revolts in Ionia

The 'burning of Sardis' is certainly the most commonly known and most sensational aspect of the Ionian Revolt. This event does little to explain the context in which the revolt occurred, nor does it give us an accurate picture of the opening chapter of open hostilities between the Greeks and Persians. The Ionian Revolt was a haphazard and uncoordinated effort that came from the opportunistic power grab by Aristagoras, *the tyrant* of Miletus.

By Dan Powers

During an attempt to take Naxos with the help of Artaphernes, then serving *satrap* of Ionia, the failed campaign to take the island began a number of intrigues and contributed to the mutual distrust between Greeks and Persians. When the joint expedition between Aristagoras of Miletus and Artaphernes failed to take Naxos, the flame of revolt was lit and fanned by Aristagoras (Herodotus 5.37). The Persians had several advantages over the Ionian Greeks who were rebelling. They had seemingly inexhaustible manpower resources and a working 'intelligence apparatus' (Herodotus; Xenophon *Anabasis, Cyropaedia, Hellenika*; Aeneas Tacticus; Polyaenus). Their navy should have been experienced and prepared, having seen recent action on the Scythian Expedition (513/2) and supporting operations in Thrace (512-510).

The attempt to take Naxos is the single incident that is cited as the justification of Persian invasions into Greece in 492 (which failed after the loss of a major naval contingent off the coast of Mount Athos on the Chalcidice Peninsula), 490, and 480. It is referenced as justification for the burning of the Acropolis in Athens (480) as well. The Persians pursued the fleeing Ionians, caught up with them near Ephesus and inflicted a defeat on the force (for more details see Fred Ray's article).

Reasons for the Ionian revolt include a number of items that are only implied by Herodotus. One is an attempt on the part of Ionian aristocracy to regain power, of course under the guise of 'freedom from Persian Control'. This is within the realm of plausibility to some degree and follows the logic of Greek aristocratic rule, which had been a staple of Ionian and other *poleis*. It also provides an underlying dissatisfaction with Persian overlord-ship.

Aristagoras began a diplomatic mission, visiting several *poleis* in Greece (500/499), in order to enlist their support for the endeavor to throw off the Persian yoke of control. The first recorded stop was at Sparta. Herodotus gives the impression that the Spartans did listen to the request for aid. The argument put forward by the historian – that there was somehow a great push for 'freedom' – is quite problematic. After some deliberation, the Spartans declined to commit assistance. Next, the instigator traveled to Athens and received hoplites as well as twenty triremes to support his effort. He also received five triremes from Eretria, on the island of Euboea, which also had very close ties to Athens. (Herodotus is less specific about the diplomatic mission of Aristagoras for additional support.)

The military side of the revolt

The revolt began in Miletus in 499. The Ionian cities of Mylasa and Termara joined with Aristagoras, and he, in turn, handed over those cities' respective tyrants to the people. Koes of Mytilene was marched out of the city and stoned to death. The

Cymeans were less harsh and released their tyrants. The first *military action* was the ad-hoc Ionian raid on Sardis that became the 'burning of Sardis.' For this venture Aristagoras had secured twenty Athenian triremes, and the five triremes from Eretria, as well as a small number of troops, presumably hoplites (for more detailed information see Fred Ray's article). Following this incident, the Athenians and Eretrians returned to their respective homes and provided no further support to the revolting Ionians.

The revolt subsequently spread from Byzantium in the north to southwest tip of Asia Minor, Caria. What we do not know is the size or locations of specific Persian garrisons in cities other than Sardis. Based on what *is* known, Ionia was only *lightly* garrisoned. The underlying theme is that Sardis had not fallen, and the *raiders* had been badly bloodied in their retreat to Ephesus. Sardis had withstood the attack and remained in Persian control. The Persian intelligence service would have informed Darius of the burning and defense simultaneously. Reinforcements could be dispatched on a more prepared timetable. Immediate reinforcements were deployed from garrisons west of the Halys River, the main body of Persian soldiers would have come overland, most likely from Gordion (Central Asia Minor) and Sinope (directly north from Gordion on the Black Sea coast). Again, details are only implied in ancient sources making the specifics difficult to determine.

In 498, the entire island of Cyprus revolted, with the exception of Amathus (a Phoenician city). It is Cyprus that sees the first major deployment of Persian forces which came from Cilicia. The major cities revolting were Salamis, Kourion, and Soloi (which was the last city to fall). As Cyprus is only 60 kilometers from the Levantine coast, such proximity to Phoenician ports, and commercial trading routes posed serious strategic risk to the Persians and the island became the obvious first priority. The revolting Cypriots quickly began to

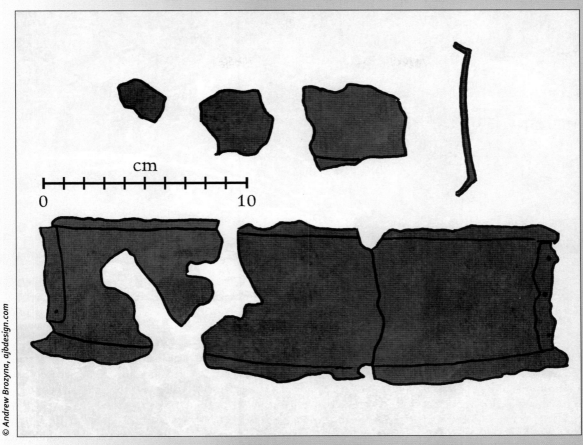

© Andrew Brozyna, ajbdesign.com

Iron nape-protector from a helmet of composite construction from Nea Paphos in Cyprus. The three fragments were found in a tunnel dug by the defenders into a siege-ramp constructed by the Persians against the city in 498 BC (after A. Jackson, 'Fragments of an Iron Helmet from Old Paphos').

besiege Amathus. The Ionian combined fleet, sent to assist the rebels, defeated a Phoenician fleet (496). Despite the victory, in which a detachment from Samos distinguished itself, the Persians landed forces on the island. The Persian land force would have headed to Amathus from its point of landing in order to relieve its single ally on the island, and on the Plains of Salamis an intense battle ensued in which many commanders on both sides were killed. This was followed by months of skirmishes, likely traversing a good portion of Cyprus, until the *polis* Kourion was betrayed by the tyrant Stesenor. The combined armies of Cyprus disintegrated, leaving only Soloi to fend off the Persian force. Onesilos, the Ionian leader on Cyprus, was killed, beheaded, and his head hung over the gates of Amathus, the one city which remained loyal to the Persians (496). Once word of Onesilos' death reached the Ionian fleet, they retreated to the Aegean. Soloi held out another several months under siege, but then was taken, ending the last resistance on Cyprus.

These events suggest some different possibilities. First that the *resistance* on

Cyprus was truly serious and skilled in its abilities, or there was a weakness in the Persian capability to answer the resistance on the battlefield, which is unlikely. Second, it is suggestive of the relatively unimportant nature the entire revolt posed to the Persian Empire as a whole. The latter would result in a *limited* military response on the part of the Persians.

While the later stage of reconquest on Cyprus was in progress, a multi-objective counterattack moved into the Ionian coastal area from the interior of Asia Minor, likely from Gordion. In the north, Persian contingents, commanded by Daurises (son in-law of Darius I), took Dardanus (497/6), while another detachment under Hymaees recaptured Chios (497?) and Sigeion (497/6). In central Ionia, Artaphernes (*satrap* of Ionia proper) and Otanes hit Cyme, Phocaea, and Clazomene in 497/6 (near Sardis). In the south, Daurises inflicted a major defeat on the Carians at their ancestral sanctuary at Labraunda in 496. Control of Caria was not entirely won, but large numbers of casualties were inflicted on the Carians. In the following year, the Carians got the

drop on Daurises' army as it moved deeper into their territory. An ambush was set up and the Persian army under Daurises was wiped out in 495 on the road outside Pedasa. That put a halt to further Persian attacks into Caria. In 496, Persian forces captured the remaining cities of the Hellespont: Abydos, Perkote, Lampsacus, and Paisos. By 496, things in Ionia had significantly changed, but not yet yielded a resolution. Aristagoras is said to have sought refuge by escaping the mess he started altogether, heading for western Thrace. During a siege at the Thracian city on the Strymon River Myrkinos in 497-6, Aristagoras was killed by Thracians.

In 496, Histaeus convinced Darius that he could turn the tide of the revolt (this man had been appointed to serve Persian interests in Thrace following the Persian campaign c. 512, and was recalled to Sardis in 499 under suspicion of creating his own empire). Darius allowed Histaeus to travel to Sardis, but Artaphrenes was suspicious of his intentions. According to Herodotus, Histaeus had ties to Aristagoras. He had tattooed a secret message on the head of a slave sent from Susa to Aristagoras,

A satrap receiving a visitor, detail of the Nereid Monument, the tomb of the ruler of Xanthos in Lycia. Now in the British Museum, London.

© Livius.org

which allegedly caused the revolt (this event is considered highly questionable by modern historians). He escaped Artaphrenes and attempted to defect to the other side. Eventually, Histaeus ended up in Byzantium without impacting events other than blockading the Euxine and commandeering ships to his side. Histaeus of Miletus (who had been released from the Persian Court to help the Persian offensive of 496) was captured near Atarneus (Thrace) and executed at Sardis by Artaphrenes in 494.

This campaign was relatively coordinated, quick, and cut the revolt into two geographically separated areas. This is effectively the same idea that was applied during the assault on Cyprus in 497. There are surviving tablets that indicate important 'intelligence' activities were ongoing and being reported to Persepolis in early 494. This indicates that by 494, Darius I, king of Persia, was intimately involved with directing resources and information to his commanders on the ground in Ionia to quell the revolt. The islands (Chios, Lesbos, Naxos, and Samos) and the mainland areas of Miletus and Caria were all isolated from any substantial help as well as cut off from communication with each other. In 494 the naval battle at Lade destroyed what was left of a combined Ionian fleet. An amphibious assault on Rhodes was conducted under the command of Datis in around in 494, though sources are not as reliable.

Preparations were now underway for a decisive fight between the rebels and the Persians. Eastern sources reveal the

likelihood that the Persians deliberately conducted a reconnaissance in order to determine the situation and how best to tackle it. Greek sources put an interesting spin on what happened, and of course no true Greek war narrative would be complete without the intervention of one, or usually several, of the Greek gods. As the Persian fleet was moving to meet with and engage the ad-hoc Ionian fleet under Histaeus, they stopped on the island of Lindos. A surviving fragment (*Fragmente der griechischen Historiker* 532.1) possibly relates that Athena got revenge on the Persians for laughing at her by giving a rain shower to the besieged populace of Lindos, thus providing for them and not the Persian force at the critical moment.

The final set piece battle occurred at Lade in 494. It seems that at this point, some six years and counting into the revolt, that Persian patience had been exhausted and all the forces available had been summoned to crush what was left of the rebels. Herodotus goes to great lengths to lay out the battle and the forces on each side with the usual inflation of numbers by Herodotus. Following the Persian naval victory, Miletus was besieged and taken. The Persian fleet wintered at Miletus and the following year (493) sailed north and subdued the last islands in the Ionian revolt (Chios, Lesbos, and Tenedos) with ease. Caria was the last area to be taken in the 'mop-up' of 493. The Persian reprisals upon the subdued cities were quite vicious. Herodotus explains Samos was the only entity to *not* be burned to the ground. "They [the Persians] picked out

the best looking boys and castrated them, the most beautiful girls were sent to the king, and the cities and temples were all burned.

The role of Persian intelligence

Often overlooked is the record of Persian 'spies' being sent to areas prior to military operations. This was a practice of Cyrus the Great, Cambyses, Darius, and the Achaemenid rulers who followed. The 'mysterious Cloak and Dagger of the Orient' is not merely a modern fascination. Information, or rather *tactical intelligence*, is not merely a modern construct, it has always had very practical uses within a military context. Darius sent such people to the Aegean Islands and mainland Greece prior to opening his campaign in 513, pursuing the European Scythians. There is in fact plenty of evidence that the administration in the Achaemenid period deliberately maintained a very active intelligence apparatus. From what information survives, it seems this part of the government was efficient and widespread. Of course, as with any such institution, it was only as useful in the extent to which its information was used. When it gave sound advice but was in turn ignored in favor of the determination of another person or group, that institution could not be summarily blamed for others' shortsightedness. Regarding the Ionian Revolt, intelligence gathering seems suspiciously absent. Perhaps the Persians did not think it necessary to maintain such information on the Ionians, though this seems unlikely. These services may have been needed for something else that was considered more important at the time, which does seem plausible. Or it may be that part of the system in that area at that time was working poorly.

The Persian military response

The resources of the Persian empire by 500 BC were immense. Considering just the Persian *satrapies* of Asia Minor, the Persians should have won outright and easily against such a small, disorganized, and less well equipped enemy. The immediate problem for the Persians was the lack of available manpower resources in Asia Minor at the outbreak of the revolt. Another issue would have been the supply line. In Persian campaigns, logistics had a serious impact on their military operations.

It is a stretch to think of the Persian military as a set 'institution' in the modern sense. Even at the height of the revolt, clearly *satrapal* contingents were the largest body in the main force. Only Xerxes' invasion of 480 resembles a state size organization. As attested by Herodotus and Xenophon's *Cyropaedia* the shift in the makeup of the Achaemenid military to a multi-lingual and multi-ethnic force as well as the corresponding challenges that came with it, parallels the expansion of Persian rule during the reign of Darius' predecessors Cyrus and Cambyses. It is unclear at what level the garrisons in Thrace continued to be maintained after the completion of Megabyzus' campaign in Thrace (480), *if* garrison forces were maintained at all. From the small amount of surviving records of Ionia, it seems Persian garrisons there were fairly small and not indicative of the norm. The reason could be that either such a military presence was not needed or other areas were far more in need of such attention, or a combination of those two reasons. This in turn may indicate that other more critical threats to the empire existed elsewhere on which information does not survive. It is clear, however, that at this time Ionia did not qualify as a direct strategic or tactical threat of any real importance to Persia.

Implications of the revolt

The Persians had so far been *politically* pragmatic about their dealings with newly conquered territories. In the broader region of Ionia, they allowed the political institutions to continue. Among Hellenic populations, the institutions of government were cresting on change. Political enfranchisement was on the rise in large ways. This is not to say that every *polis* had become a *functioning democracy* overnight, but significant changes were in the air by 510. By the year 500, in the extreme cases there was a functioning democracy. The most obvious example is Athens, but large numbers of Ionians were still closely related to Athens, and the Ionian Revolt very clearly demonstrates the close ties were still in place.

Second is the economic impact due to enforcement of stringent trade regulations by the Persian central government which probably reduced the commercial activities of Ionia. This would have restricted Ionian Greeks from participating in trans-Mediterranean trade at all, leaving Phoenicians with a monopoly. There is evidence of a marked decline in artistic production as well as trade in finished products. One theory postulates that this trend clearly shows Persian Royal preferential treatment of the Phoenician interests. It may also reveal an internal political fear of the peoples not closely associated with the Achaemenid core administration. The Persian bureaucracy might have seen the Phoenicians as far less of a threat politically or militarily to their rule than Greeks with 'questionable ties' to other outsiders. That would have given the Persians less incentive to fully incorporate the Greeks into their system. This had practical elements that must have been considered by Darius and his governing administration. The unintended consequence of this approach was that it rapidly alienated Ionian populations and pushed them away in all senses from the ruling powers. The Aegean Greeks had just been regulated out of direct competition with the Phoenicians who already had an advantage in their ancestral ties with the Carthaginians. This decline in economic monopolies may have helped to provide serious economic difficulties that directly impacted the socio-economic status of ruling classes in all of the Greek *poleis*.

Third, a major factor may be something that is not directly recorded. The response to the spread of the revolt was fairly slow and never included a campaign attended by Darius himself. Without faulting Darius too much, the idea has been put forward that the Ionian Revolt was small and not a major event for the Persians. This explains why the Persian response was small. This idea would then indicate that the revolt was considered only slightly more than a minor risk. With a limited response on the part of the Persians, putting down even a small revolt would require a longer amount of time, energy, and money. This is plausible and also offers a possible explanation as to why the revolt was able to last over six years into 493. It also provide an indication that other more pressing matters were occurring elsewhere in the empire; things far more important than the area of Ionia. (Sadly evidence of these outside threats to Persia in this period do not survive or have yet to be discovered). It also raises an important question: How much control did the Persians actually exercise over their empire? It does indicate that their control was far more tenuous than they wanted outsiders to believe.

Fleets and logistics

The Persian Royal Road system arced northwest from the capital at Susa through Gordion and then turned southwest terminating in Sardis. The road went through a number of mountain passes, which would cause significant problems in maintaining large quantities of supplies. Once the Persian fleet had finished supporting the operation on Cyprus, it was then free to move into the Aegean. Although not completely safe, the fleet was able to provide additional supply support to the Persian forces operating in Ionia. The Persian counterstrikes to the areas of the western coast were relatively limited and time consuming. As time, progressed the combined Ionian fleet would have had to split into smaller sections as each respective contingent would have needed to maintain itself closer and closer to its home port to protect it from Persian reprisals. That, in turn, provided successively easier victories for the Persian fleet. Once the Persian fleet entered the Aegean, it would also have caused substantial problems for Ionian communication thus disrupting military coordination between the Ionian allies.

© Karwansaray Publishers

An aryballos, *a container for perfumes and unguents, in the shape of a so-called Ionian helmet. Though never attested archaeologically, the type is distinctive in its lack of a nasal protector, the shape of the brow and a ridge front to back. Now in the Louvre, Paris.*

areas than they were in others, but it does provide credibility to the organizational talent of Darius as well as his respective governors in Asia Minor in this period. The entire incident helps to set the tone of mistrust and demonization by both Greeks and Persians alike towards one another politically, militarily, and culturally. If the campaign of Darius into Scythia serves as the metaphorical prologue to the clash of these two civilizations, the Ionian Revolt is more than a beginning footnote, more appropriately it serves as Chapter One of the great conflict. ●

Dan Powers recently finished his BA studies in Ancient History and will begin his formal graduate studies focusing on Greek Warfare. He currently is Secretary of the Society of Ancient Military Historians and a former career soldier who has operated extensively around the world.

Conclusion

The Ionian Revolt is a pivotal point in both Hellenic and Persian history. It provides an interesting insight into the practical functioning of Achaemenid institutions, and international tensions that plagued the interaction of east and west. It provides a few snapshots that allow some cursory analysis of the Persian army and government organizations under Darius. The length of time required to eradicate the revolt, which seems to have been mostly a collection of spontaneous responses to political and possibly economic threats, indicates that the Persians were not particularly adept at resolving conflict with military force. Their access to seemingly inexhaustible resources appears to be the reason the Persians were able to win in the end. The fact that it took a year (or close to) to resolve just the Cypriot revolt raises critical suspicions about the efficacy of the

Persian military machine. Such evidence also denies the notion of a 'Persian Navy'.

The fact that they were, in the end, able to marshal those resources and how they dealt with the rebellious cities once the revolt had been suppressed, enhances the analysis of Persian ability to conduct excellent government and specifically the political and organizational talent of Darius. Largely in response to the pressures of governance, Mardonius, in command of a Persian army the year after calm is restored, forcibly deposed aristocratic Greek governments and imposed democratic councils in the <I>poleis<I> on the Ionian coast. This certainly gives insight into the sensitivity the Persians had in general terms to the concepts of good governance and an adeptness at understanding how to allow releases of political pressures to prevent outright revolts. The Persians were better at this in some

Further reading

- P. Briant, *From Cyrus to Alexander, A History of the Persian Empire*. Ann Arbor, MI 2002.
- F. Dvornik, *Origins of Intelligence Services*. Piscataway, NJ 1974.
- K. Farrokh, *Shadows in the Desert, Ancient Persia at War*. Oxford 2007.
- I. Gershevitch (ed.), *Cambridge History of Iran, Volume 2, The Median and Achaemenian Periods*. Cambridge 1985.
- A. Kuhrt, *The Persian Empire, A Corpus of Sources from the Achaemenid Period*. London and New York 2007.
- M. Sheldon, *Espionage in the Ancient World, an annotated bibliography*. Jefferson, NC 2008.
- H.T. Wallinga, 'The Ancient Persian Navy and its Predecessors', in: H. Sancisi-Weedenburg (ed.), *Predecessors in Achaemenid History I, The Greek Sources Structures and Synthesis, proceedings of the Groningen 1983 Achaemenid History Workshop*. Leiden 1987.

The battle of Ephesus – 498 BC
Prelude to Marathon

The epic struggle between the Grecian city-states and the mighty Persian Empire that found its signature moment in Athens' famed underdog victory over an invading army at Marathon did not begin there on the coastal plain of Attica. Rather, its roots lie years earlier and far away on the other side of the Aegean. Here it was the Athenians who had landed from the sea as invaders, and it was *their* now much lauded combat system that went down to an inglorious defeat on the home ground of a very different way of war.

By Fred Eugene Ray

This is the story of the battle of Ephesus, a tale that at best garners little more than passing mention in most military histories. Nonetheless, our chronicle of the Persian Wars begins with events surrounding this episode; and it was their loss at Ephesus that labeled Athens' warriors as underdogs at Marathon. It was also there where the Athenians gained vital tactical lessons that would key their and other Greeks' later successes over Persian arms.

A grand diversion

Led by the city of Miletus, Greeks on the islands and across the coastal region of Anatolia (modern Turkey) had gone into revolt against the Persian Empire in 499 (see Dan Powers's article in this issue) and sought aid from their European kin. While Sparta had rejected their appeal, Athens was more receptive. Its decision to join in this enterprise had close links with the city's legendary role as homeland of the Asian Greeks. Indeed, the loose terms 'Ionians' and 'Ionia' for these people and their region derive from a tradition that they came from the vicinity of Athens with its Ionian brand of the Greek language. These settlers actually spoke many dialects signaling multiple origins; nevertheless, the myth of Ionian Athens as founder had strong appeal on both sides of the Aegean. Yet simple kinship wasn't the only

thing on Athenian minds in tendering aid. Athens had become a democracy little more than a decade earlier after ejecting its last tyrant, Hippias, who had fled to the Persian court where he had been lobbying for help in a return to power. Boosting the insurrection was a way for the Athenians to divert support for Hippias by keeping his Persian friends busy in their own backyard.

The expeditionary force

Twenty Athenian warships under Melanthios set off for Ionia in the spring of 498 along with five vessels from Eretria on the large island of Euboa just off the east coast of Greece. Herodotus' details on this flotilla give us our only hard clues on probable size of the mainland Greek expeditionary force. The ships were undoubtedly all triremes (*trieres*), a type of oared galley of Corinthian or Phoenician origin that was far and away the dominant warship design throughout the entire 5th century (and much of the 4th as well). Tightly packed with 170 rowers sitting along three tiers in addition to 16 deck hands, these sleek naval engines were extremely fast in battle. On the down side, their speed-conscious construction and large complement of oarsmen left only very limited space for cargo of any sort, including passengers. Much of what is known today about the

latter comes down to us from the Troizen Inscription of the late 4th to early 3rd centuries; however, this in fact dealt with rather unique Athenian ships that were built under Themistocles as a response to the Persian seaborne threat connected with the battle of Marathon nearly a decade after the subject period. These vessels were optimal for maneuver warfare; relying on ram-equipped prows and having only partial decking, they carried no more than fourteen marines (ten spearmen and four archers). This made them quite different from the fully decked versions of the trireme that would have been in use at the time of the Ionian Revolt (as well as the decked-over triremes to which the Athenians would revert later in the century, when they had come to be more concerned with amphibious operations). Older designs relevant to our Ephesus calculations commonly boasted much larger numbers of fighting men on board, which in this era sought to contend in hand-to-hand combats across the adjacent decks of opposing ships.

Based upon a note by Herodotus on what seems to have been an unusually large load of marines that served aboard Grecian ships from the island of Chios during the battle of Lade, it's quite likely that 40 hoplite heavy spearmen was close to the maximum troop allotment that a completely decked trireme could carry. Accordingly, we can reasonably project that the force that crossed over to join in the Ionian Revolt might very well have consisted of somewhere around 1,000 hoplites: 800 Athenian and 200 from Eritrea. These reinforcements joined with local rebels once in Asian waters and their combined fleets then put in at Ephesus, which was a major Grecian center on the central Ionian coast some 50km north of Miletus.

The Persian garrison

Persia's king Darius had not stood entirely idle in the face of this developing situation and seems to have organized a modest military force over the winter of 499/498 to restore order in Ionia. He apparently crafted this out of standing garrisons from his provinces (*satrapies*) west of the Halys River (along the interior Lydian border) and thus nearest the rebellion. The resulting army might have been based around two divisions of royal infantry, possibly one from each of the satrapies of Sardis (former Lydian territory) and *Tyaiy Drayahya* ("Those of the Sea", south of the Euxine/Black Sea and east of Sardis). These same units would also have served two other provinces: Skudra (Thrace and Macedonia) and Caria (south and east of Ionia). There appears to have been a third such garrison division in the west at the moment, posted below Caria along the south coast of Asia Minor within the satrapy of Cilicia. However, risk of yet more trouble on nearby Cyprus (where a revolt would indeed break out within the year) meant that these troops had to stay put.

Royal divisions of foot (called "myriads" by the Greeks and maybe *baivaraba* in Persian) were ordered by tens. Each contained ten regiments (*hazaraba*) of ten companies (*sataba*) with ten squads (*dathaba*) apiece. Since a squad (*dathabam*) had ten men, this yielded a nominal manpower of 10,000 per division. However, surviving accounting records suggest that actual or 'parade' strength might have been around 80% of nominal if a unit was newly mustered and only 30-60% when on lengthy garrison duty like those utilized during the Ionian Revolt. The Persians adjusted for this by fielding squads at a full count of ten while cutting the number of them in a company to fit the complement on hand - only five squads per company if at 50% of nominal for example. Therefore, the host dealing with the unrest in Ionia likely had no more than 12,000 Persian footmen (60% nominal). All of these troops would have come from the empire's core 'Iranian' citizenry (Persians, Medes, Elamites/Cissians/Kashshites and Hyrkanians) and had ideally trained in military arts (riding and weaponry) from the age of five to twenty, after which they were liable for four years of duty in the imperial garrisons (or as royal guards for those of high birth). From age 25 to 50 they then could be called upon to staff the officer corps or serve as veterans in large campaigns of conquest requiring more manpower than the regular standing garrisons could provide.

Normally forming a linear combat array one *dathabam* deep and spaced at about 1m per file, these troops of the line were known as *sparabara* (shield-bearers). This was because at least the first man in each file held a large, rectangular, wicker shield or *spara*. He used this along with those of his mates on either side to create a barrier screen at the front, which he and those immediately behind could defend as needed with a short (2m), thrusting spear fitted with a rounded counterweight to allow for greater reach through a grip farther back on the shaft. Within its 'shield-wall,' most of the formation was free to operate as bowmen to arc a dense cloud of arrows onto the opposition. Whether plying shield and/or spear at the fore or bow farther back, each man in this mixed arms arrangement carried a straight sword (*akinakes*) as a secondary weapon. As for defensive gear, it was minimal. All wore soft headdresses and, save possibly for a few officers, had no body armor.

Cavalrymen with javelins (some perhaps with bows as well) rode on the edges of the *sparabara* formation. So effective were these mounted troops and their light-armed foot support that the flanks of Persian arrays were seldom at hazard, thus putting greater emphasis on the center of the infantry, where it was customary to station the army's best soldiers. Satrapal riders came from among privileged Persians holding local fiefs (termed 'bow-land') in return for providing cavalry duty upon demand. There would have been some 1,600 horsemen present at one regiment (*hazarabam*) of 800 (at 80% of nominal) per garrison. Their supporting skirmishers were provincial foreign levies, called together in this case from those remaining loyal within the western satrapies. These most probably consisted of a Mysian division. The Mysians were light-armed foot soldiers with short, throwing spears, helmets and small shields. This contingent would have been a local draft, possibly on the order of 8,000 strong (again, 80% of an authorized *baivarabam*-sized unit). In addition to these light footmen, a native levy of Lydian infantry was undoubtedly present as well. (In fact, these were apparently well used to working as a team with the nearby Mysians as indicated by the two nationalities combining to form a single brigade within the host of Xerxes in 480.) The Lydians were armored foot-

men very similar to the Greeks' hoplites, though their spears seem to have been a bit shorter than the 2.5m Grecian norm. Addition of both the Lydians and Mysians would have brought the host up to nearly 30,000 combatants

The campaign

Herodotus' account, our primary source on the Ionian Revolt, is somewhat vague and disjointed on occasion, jumping around enough to sometimes obscure relative timing of events and give rise to reasonable differences of opinion on the proper sequence. With that caveat in mind, it's proposed here that the imperials set out for Ionia while Greek resistance was still forming and, under three of Darius' sons-in-law (Daurises, Hymaees and Otanes), marched on the rebellion's epicenter at Miletus. Plutarch said that the Persians then invested that peninsular location, seemingly settling in for a landward siege to take out the foremost hostile citadel right away. This turned out to be a difficult task, since Miletus was a port well able to supply itself from the sea. (In fact, the city would hold out until taken by storm in the winter of 494/493 only after a major naval reverse had weakened its seaborne line of support.)

The Greeks at Ephesus now looked to go on the offensive. Their strength in heavy infantry might have come to about 6,000 hoplites, judging that the military and social organizations of most Greek city-states ran in close parallel. The Milesians Hermophantos and Charopinos (brother of Aristogoras, the city's leader) had therefore likely brought around 2,000 of these soldiers equipped with a long, steel-tipped spear with butt-spike, a heavy shield of wood thinly sheathed in bronze and both a brazen helmet and body armor of metal (greaves) and leather or stiffened linen (about the torso). This was a two-thirds levy, as was common for Greek armies serving outside their own territory, which counted four 500-man regiments or *lochoi* out of a probable six available (one *lochos* for each of the city's recorded tribal elements – four of them Ionian [Aigikoreis, Hopletes, Geleontes and Argadeis] and two drawn from the local native population). Ephesus, very likely standing in joint command on home soil, could well have matched the contribution from Miletus. This might have been about all that the city could spare for an extended stay in the field if it was to maintain sufficient defensive capability. The remaining Greek heavy footmen consisted of the trireme-borne Athenians and Eretrians, with possibly another 1,000 hoplites provided by a mix of smaller Ionian contingents.

The rebels' sizeable collection of armored spearmen made for quite a powerful force by Grecian standards; its strength, however, lay entirely in hand-to-hand or 'shock' fighting. The uprising was short on missile firepower, there being no cavalry assets of any note and maybe only about 1,000 amateur foot skirmishers (*psiloi*) on hand (representing a combatant minority from among the army's large gang of baggage handlers). These agile troops carried a bundle of short and slender javelins that they could hurl out to a considerable distance. With this sort of reach, they had potential to offer a significant threat to javelin-armed horsemen, whose weapon range could have been only half as far. And though this was a somewhat lesser problem for those Persian riders of this period that also carried longer reaching bows, even these would have to be seriously concerned for their horses, which made large and inviting targets. All the same, the Greek *psiloi* lacked armor and, perhaps, even shields (their protection might have consisted of no more than a cloak wrapped about the left arm). They therefore had little ability to scrap at close quarters, which combined with their modest numbers here to make the prospect of openly tackling the larger and more versatile Persian host a highly risky proposition. The rebellion's leaders therefore picked out a softer mark: the satrapal capital at Sardis. This city, sitting some 75km to the northeast, was for the moment only weakly defended, having lent most of its troops to the effort around Miletus. A successful strike at so prominent a site would not only score a major propaganda coup, but might well draw the Persians away from Miletus.

The Greek army marched rapidly on Sardis, driving the satrap Artaphernes and his small garrison into refuge. However, things soon deteriorated as fires set in this metropolis of thatched roofs and reed huts blazed into a holocaust that claimed much of the city. Driven by smoke, flame and rapidly rising resistance to relocate south of town, the rebels then discovered that the diversionary aspect of their attack had succeeded all too well. Reacting with

A Greek hoplite and his servant – in front – on the march. The light infantry, when not specialists such as the Thracians, may often have consisted of lightly armored servants. Note that he, apart from a variety of containers, is wearing a helmet, while the hoplite carries a Corinthian helmet and his own aspis. Second half of the fifth century BC, now in the Louvre, Paris.

surprising speed and unity, the trio of Persian commanders already had a relief force on its way with perhaps all their cavalry and half the available infantry. This meant that the Greeks had to withdraw at once if they were to avoid engaging on unfavorable ground far from a friendly base. Decamping in haste, they made for Ephesus with the enemy close behind.

Deployment for battle

The rebels moved down along the Cayster River and eventually crossed to turn and face their pursuers on the floodplain immediately northeast of Ephesus. It was a location that put them on flat and open terrain well suited to their style of shock-centric combat, letting their left flank anchor next to the river while the *psiloi* in their entirety covered the right end of the battle line. The Greek phalanx was a closely ordered, linear affair that featured hoplites in long ranks of adjoining shields, with files stacking as circumstance dictated. Most of the time, phalanxes tried to stand around eight men deep; a com-

A mix of armored Anatolian and Persian cavalry, supported by light infantry delivered the crucial blow after an exhausting barrage of missiles. While most of the line still held, one flank started to give way, triggering a rout.

© Giorgio Albertin

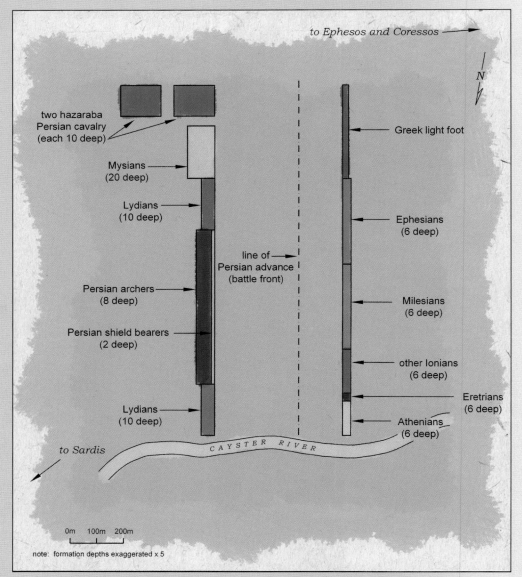

two hazaraba
Persian cavalry
(each 10 deep)

Mysians
(20 deep)

Lydians
(10 deep)

line of
Persian advance
(battle front)

Persian archers
(8 deep)

Persian shield bearers
(2 deep)

Lydians
(10 deep)

to Sardis

CAYSTER RIVER

to Ephesos and Coressos

N

Greek light foot

Ephesians
(6 deep)

Milesians
(6 deep)

other Ionians
(6 deep)

Eretrians
(6 deep)

Athenians
(6 deep)

0m   100m   200m

note: formation depths exaggerated x 5

Projected deployments at the battle of Ephesus.

unanchored left flank. They would have done this in conjunction with the Persian cavalry, with which they needed to coordinate for both the latter's protection as well as to bolster attacks against opposing skirmishers along that side of the field.

For their part, the rebels would have stationed the Ephesian troops on their right wing, this being a post of honor traditionally held by those fighting at home, with the Milesians standing throughout the center of the phalanx. The remaining, lesser Ionian contingents probably came next in order, followed by the spearmen from Eretria and, finally, the Athenians to complete the left wing all the way to the river's edge.

Battle is joined

Coming up into bow range, the Persians would have stopped to present their shield-wall; they then began to rain a punishing barrage of arrows upon the rebels. Taking this stoically at first behind stout shields and armor, the Greeks had little choice in the end but to pick their way forward through the deadly fall of missiles until they could engage hand-to-hand and shelter their foremost ranks from archery within the enemy formation's own shadow. The resulting melee then presumably stalled as the Lydians and Persian front-fighters with shields kept the hoplites at bay, fending off spear thrusts and absorbing whatever weakened and, perhaps, poorly coordinated pressure (*othismos*) the Greeks could muster from their thin formation. All the while, *sparabara* bowmen continued to wound the phalanx's rearward ranks, their shafts piercing thighs, upper arms and throats with cruelly barbed heads that

promise which gave good width of rank while still keeping enough depth of file for both orderly marching and effective pushing against the opposition (see Paul Bardunias' article in this issue).

As it turned out, the Greeks at Ephesus must have lined up thinner than usual (maybe only six deep) that they could better prevent being outflanked on their right. This was because the Persian army that now arrived to form up in opposition to the east was able to spread out its line infantry over a full kilometer width. Such a deployment assumes that the imperials' dominant approach of basing their combat formation around a forward shield-wall required them to set up the *sparabara* in the middle of their battle line. Given the likelihood that this was part of a standard

symmetrical formation design, the heavy-armed Lydians must then have split into two contingents in order to take post on either side of the Persians (Plutarch's description of the preliminary action at the battle of Plataea in 479 seems to support this arrangement. The Lydians had similarly deployed with *sparabara* against a phalanx in that action and apparently held the same kind of wing position. In this case, they seem to have been nearest the enemy commander, who almost surely stood somewhere toward the rightward extreme of the Spartan array). All of these troops of the line probably filed ten deep (one *dathabam* or the equivalent) in accordance with usual custom and their lowest level organization. As for the Mysians, they must have taken position off the

Greek warriors fighting a mounted Persian. The latter is shown wearing typically eastern style clothing with tunic, trousers, shoes and a soft-skin hat. The hoplite is shown heroically nude apart from his helmet, while the archer, barely visible to his rear, only wears a tunic. Approximately 360-330 BC, now in the British Museum, London.

badly for the Greeks. Nor did things improve in the uprising's ensuing months and years. In fact, Darius' armies took battle after battle from hoplite foes, losing but a single ambush prior to putting effective end to the Ionian Revolt with a crushing naval victory at Lade. Thoroughly discouraged, the Athenians gave up the war for good after Ephesus, yet had learned a great deal from that painful experience. Never again would they so greatly expose a flank to cavalry on open ground; never again would they stand with an entire line thinned to match a Persian front; and never again would they endure for so long under missile fire before charging on the run to put *sparabara* to the spear. These teachings came to bear with decisive impact just a few years later, when the Persians came to avenge the burning of Sardis and Athens' spearmen would save their city, and perhaps western civilization as well, in a brilliant triumph at Marathon. •

Fred Eugene Ray is author of Land Battles in 5th Century B.C. Greece: A History and Analysis of 173 Engagements (McFarland and Company, 2009) and is working on a similar study for the 4th century. A former petroleum industry exploration geologist and executive, he lives and works in Bakersfield, California, USA.

tore flesh all the more upon any attempt to remove them.

Such a stalemate couldn't have gone on for too long and it most likely was the cavalry and Mysian light foot of the Persian left wing that delivered the crucial blow. Exhausting *psiloi* javelins in a series of charge-and-retreat attacks, these imperials must have burst forward at that point to scatter the now nearly defenseless Greek skirmishers. They next wheeled around the freshly exposed enemy right, hitting the Ephesians fighting there from both side and rear. It was more than these troops could reasonably bear and they broke, many tossing away their shields as all ran for their lives. This sent a rapid collapse rushing down the phalanx from right to left, with hoplites falling to assaults on their unshielded right as each fleeing man exposed his neighbor on that side.

When the last of the Ionians had given way, Lydian spearmen on the Persian rightward wing moved to roll up the hoplites from Eritrea, whose commander, Eualcidas, was probably among the first to die. Standing in the accustomed general's post forward on the right, this famous athlete and a goodly number of his soldiers went down before the rest of the Euboans joined their Athenian allies in a mad rush down the river to the nearby harbor and a timely ship-borne escape. Having taken crippling losses and with its allies fled, Ephesus soon had no option but to surrender.

Aftermath

This first real contest between the Greek and Persian ways of war thus ended very

Further reading:

- A.R. Burn, *Persia and the Greeks*. London 1984.
- M. Grant, *The Rise of the Greeks*. New York 1987.
- R. Nelson, *Armies of the Greek and Persian Wars 500-350 B.C.* Goring-by-Sea, Sussex 1975.
- F.E. Ray, *Land Battles in 5th Century B.C. Greece*. Jefferson, N.C. 2009.
- N. Sekunda and S. Chew, *The Persian Army 560-330 BC*. London 1992.

The Persians cross the Aegean
Marathon dawn

To the Greeks, if there was one defining event in their history, it was the Persian Wars. Of the two most famous battles during the first decades of the fifth century BC, Marathon is remembered as the event that saved a budding democracy and defended the classic Greek philosophy, art and culture which contributed so mightily to later Western thought and culture.

By Ronald Ruiters

For this was ten years before Thermopylae, Salamis and Plataea, where the Greeks would prove the valour of their hoplites, the effectiveness of their phalanx tactics and, that when united, there was no greater power in the known world. These were relatively untested forces whose experience rested mainly on fighting other Greeks (except for those who had fought as mercenaries in the service of the Egyptians or, ironically, for the Persians).

For the fractious Greeks, Marathon was a metaphorical re-enactment of the campaign against Troy in which their ancestors united under the Mycenaean king to fight the barbarian East. Bethany Hughes has pointed out that, among others, both the playwright Aeschylus, a veteran of Marathon, and Herodotus drew an imaginary fault line between East and West with the Trojan War 'story' as a "political and cultural polemic" (Hughes 2005).

From a practical point of view, the Greeks (particularly the Athenians) had two strategic concerns. The first was Persian expansion. For the Greeks, fifth century Persia was the sole super-power in their world. In landmass alone, the Achaemid Empire covered 7.5 million square miles and, as argued elsewhere in this issue, had vast amounts of many resources. The Greeks' second, and perhaps more crucial strategic issue was the protection of the grain route from the Black Sea. Both led to Athens' (and Eretria's) support for the revolt of the Ionian Greeks – 499 - 493 BC. Darius' failed offensive into Lydia had encouraged the Ionians and the Athenians to take advantage of the Persian's distraction there.

The 'false start' in 492

For their part, Persian strategic goals were clear. Darius was not simply bent on revenge for the burning of Sardis and Athenian complicity. He was too practical to embark on an offensive that would only be an expensive distraction. This was a dangerous period for the Achaemids, with constant revolt against the empire demanding constant vigilance. Darius was seeking to secure his empire from further revolts, and from the interference of the mainland Greeks. This created a necessity for him to set an example to the empire – this was not so much pure revenge as exemplary punishment.

The Persians aimed at achieving their objectives by the most economic means. What would become in fact the first Persian invasion of Greece began in 492 BC, with the Persian general Mardonius (Darius's son-in-law) conquering Thrace and Macedon. Lacey (2011) argues that this was not originally a prelude to an immediate assault, but itself designed to set up a secure base for future offensive operations onto the Attic mainland.

A series of mishaps spelled disaster for Mardonius' force, particularly a violent storm (or series of storms) along the Thracian mainland off Mount Athos. Herodotus tells us that the Persians lost 300 ships and over 20,000 men. Mardonius, who was himself injured, returned to Persia where his father-in-law – Darius - sacked him. Over a decade later, the same Mardonius led Darius' son's (Xerxes) second invasion of Greece in 480 BC (perhaps proving that family connections counted).

Tile from Toumba (Thessaloniki), in northern Greece, attesting to the presence of Persian soldiers. The graffito shows someone wearing a tiara and holding spear, shield or scepter. The text is in one of the alphabets in use in the Persian empire.

© Karwansaray Publishers

Thracian soldiers, recognizable by their headdress, carrying a deep, bowled shield and a pair of (throwing?) spears. From the Apadana, the audience hall, of Darius' palace at Persepolis. Now in the Pergamon Museum, Berlin, Germany.

The Persian campaign of 490

Almost all the primary sources for the Greco-Persian Wars are Greek. There are no surviving historical narratives from the Persian side. By some distance, the main source for the Greco-Persian Wars is the Greek historian Herodotus. As Holland says, obviously admiringly: "For the first time, a chronicler set himself to trace the origins of a conflict not to a past so remote so as to be utterly fabulous, nor to the whims and wishes of some god, nor to a people's claim to manifest destiny, but rather explanations he could verify personally."

Between the false start of 492 and 490, both the Athenians and Spartans rejected the usual demands for Earth and Water, making them virtually alone amongst the Greeks as a whole. In 490 BC, a second force was sent to Greece, this time across the Aegean Sea, under the joint command of Datis and Artaphernes. This offensive would avoid the Thracian land route.

Contrary to many Hollywood and popular fiction depictions of the Persians, the Empire and its forces were a world-class organization. The East was the 'cradle of war'. Persian kings – like their Babylonian,

Mede and Assyrian predecessors – were expected to be war leaders – to expand their empires by force (or at least by the threat of force). Their operational planning was meticulous and revolutionary. Herodotus indicates that the Persians, far from operating with the alleged Oriental thoughtlessness, followed highly prepared staff plans, even though they were hampered by a certain rigidity in execution.

As it happened, the Persians had decided to experiment with completely different tactics. Instead of using the navy to support a large land army, the navy would be used as the main instrument of attack. The year 491 BC was spent in putting together and training an army that was not-too-great by Persian standards, but nonetheless a formidable force of infantry and cavalry which was to be carried by the fleet and used in amphibious operations. The triremes, which were in the usual number of 600, carried the infantry. The cavalry was carried on other triremes that had been specially adapted for that purpose.

The force sailed from Cilicia first to the island of Rhodes, where a Lindian Temple Chronicle records that Datis besieged the

city of Lindos, but was unsuccessful. The fleet sailed next to Naxos, to punish the Naxians for their resistance to the failed expedition the Persians had mounted there a decade earlier, burning the city and temples of the Naxians. The fleet then proceeded to Eretria, taking hostages and troops from each island.

The first major target, Eretria was razed after a seven-day siege and the temples and shrines were looted and burned. The Persians enslaved all the remaining townspeople.

The Persians intended to conduct amphibious operations and land the army at a suitable bridgehead on the inhospitable coastline. There was not much to choose from. Their marine reconnaissance found one that offered good ground, just large enough to accept the landing. Their choice was at Marathon.

Greek intelligence for the campaign

The Persians were engaged in a new kind of warfare – what we call an amphibious operation. Up until that moment, the Athenians could not have guessed what they were up against. Herodotus reports that the people of Eretria became aware of the Persian plans against them only after the enemy had landed on their island.

There are few records that describe the intelligence available to the Greek force at Marathon Bay. The historical record leaves us enough to describe the battle and the events before and after with as much clarity as any report 2500 years later can give us. Anthropological and particularly geo-military analysis, helps us construct a plausible sequence of events. We know that the Greeks were on their own soil. Since there were few – and therefore obvious landing sites – the Athenians would have detected the Persian reconnaissance parties quickly. The Persians were a large force composed of a variety units. Command and control would be difficult and, if we believe Herodotus, driven by whips and fear. Stealth was not an option or a concern for the Persians. This was a force that hadn't experienced defeat in recent memory. The Persian presence would have been loud and brazen. Psychology played a great part in Persian tactics. Their demands for Earth and Water from their enemies – traditional tokens of submission- were the easy avoidance of battle for their enemies.

© Livius.org

The King of Kings, Darius I of Persia, from the northern stairs of the apadana of Darius' palace at Persepolis. Now in the Archaeological Museum, Tehran, Iran.

are the land breeze and the sea breeze. The land breeze usually begins to blow during the night and stops around dawn.

The Persian Force: The Persian forces were a diverse group, but with general conformity in armor and style of fighting. In the Greco-Persian wars, both sides made use of spear-armed infantry and light missile troops. While Greek armies placed the emphasis on heavier infantry, Persian armies favored lighter troop types. The troops on the Persian side were usually armed with a bow, a relatively short spear and a sword or axe, and carried wicker shields. They wore a variety of armor, usually of organic materials, although individuals of high stature wore high quality metal armor. They were highly reliant on their bowmen and used their cavalry to ride down enemy flanks.

Greek preparations for defense

In many ways, conditions for a Greek victory were in place. Any reasonable assessment makes it clear that as long as Athens stayed on the strategic defensive, the deck was not as stacked against her as typically assumed.

Numbers: Athens had complete warning of the Persian offensive. It was also after the harvest - maximizing available manpower. In an emergency (such as at Marathon), Athens could mobilize the lower class and if necessary slaves (normally forbidden), likely as slingers and skirmishers. It is generally agreed that the Athenians were heavily outnumbered, though by what factor is debated (see also the next article). Given the strength of the defense and by correlating terrain and other battlefield as well as moral and psychological advantages, it can be reckoned that a ratio of at least three to one and up to five to one of offensive versus defensive forces was required for victory. That was certainly not the case, as it turned out.

To the Persians, the 'Ionians across the sea' were a fractious, and relatively unimportant foreign people on the periphery of the Empire. For their part, the Greeks knew the Persians. Greek mercenaries had fought on both sides in Persian and Egyptian campaigns far from Attica. Many, like Miltiades, who played a key role at Marathon, had actually held land holdings under Persian suzerainty.

Intelligence Preparation of the Battlespace (IPB) has been conducted in a relatively unchanged fashion through the ages. There are three main aspects to that preparation: terrain, weather and enemy forces. The first two – weather and terrain are 'neutral.' The latter includes knowledge about enemy force's strategy, tactics, weapons and doctrine. Greek IPB would have told them the following:

Terrain: The plain of Marathon was limited to the north by a large lagoon and to the south by a smaller one and was further cut by fast moving rivers and streams, restricting the Persian army to a relatively small area. The Persians chose a location where they could easily defend themselves if they were attacked while landing their cavalry. Furthermore, the long sandy beach of Marathon would permit them to pull their triremes on shore. This would have been necessary in order

to discharge the horses from the triremes, which must have been a long and complex operation. The time needed to disembark and embark the horses may have been the greatest single cause of failure in the campaign of Marathon.

Time: Time played a key factor in Persian – and Greek – planning. While it allowed the Persians to consolidate their beachhead, each day was a logistical challenge. The Persian army could literally only travel with its supply column close behind. That column was reliant on the sea. Also, the beach accommodated only a portion of the army and the ships; if they were all pulled on shore with edges of their decks touching, the triremes would have required about a three kilometer strip of beach!

Weather: The Persians would have studied the ordinary pattern of the winds and currents with care. The flow of the winds on the southwest side of Euboea and in the Sardonic Gulf is quite different from that of the rest of Greece, because the mountainous rib of Euboea deflects the Etesian winds, blowing from the northern quadrant. As a result of this deflection, winds are particularly strong to the east side of Euboea but unimportant to the west of it. To the southwest of Euboea and in the Saronic Gulf, the winds that count

Iron sword from the Achaemenid era. Now in the Tehran Archaeological Museum, Tehran, Iran.

© Livius.org

It has been argued that in many ways, the Greek force at Marathon was a veteran force. This is a key point – in many ways, Athens was a nation at arms. They had been at constant war for the past twenty years and had defeated Thebes, Calchis, Aegina and Sparta.

The style of warfare between the Greek city-states, which dates back to at least 650 BC, was based around the hoplite phalanx supported by missile troops. The Greek hoplite – with his *aspis*, wearing armor and bearing a nine-foot long hardened iron-tipped spear and a forged iron sword – was the most effective fighting man of his time. The phalanx in which he fought and the shield wall in which he stood, fought and died became the classic Western way of war for centuries. Philip of Macedon modified and perfected it and his son Alexander used it to destroy an empire and change cultures. The phalanx could only be defeated by another phalanx... or cavalry. There lay a potential rub: Persian cavalry, added to the navy, completed the principle of absolute mobility on which the strategy of the Persian operation was founded. There are critical historians who claim that Herodotus' mention of a Persian cavalry force carried on triremes fitted for the transport of horses is preposterous. They state it would have been impossible to transport horses on a long sea voyage, a claim that can easily be laid aside. In 415 BC, the Athenians were to sail to Syracuse in Sicily with a force of 100 triremes fitted out for naval combat and carrying 4000 hoplites and 300 horses.

Miltiades, who by most accounts led the Greek force at Marathon, followed the strategy recommended by the best German generals 2500 years later when the Allies were planning their 1944 landing in France: one should try to stop the Allies within the first two kilometers from the shore or not try at all. The Athenians set up camp at the very margin of the plain of Marathon in an area that was higher and rocky, so that the Persians could not use their cavalry against them. The Athenians aligned themselves across the valley of Vrana, the very bottom of which is about 2000 meters from the shore of Marathon. The Persians were aligned along the shore in front of their ships that were either beached or moored on the sandy beach in the bay of Marathon. The result of this extremely daring maneuver by Miltiades was that the Persians could not move from

their position. They had landed in Attica but they had found themselves pinned against the shore. Their strength was the cavalry but they could not use it against the Greek positions, and if they tried to move either north or south along the shore they would be exposed to a flank attack. If they tried to embark their forces, they could be exposed to an attack while they were in disarray. The infantry could be embarked quickly, but the embarking of the horses must have been a lengthy operation.

The Sanctuary of Herakles at the inland base of the plain anchored the Greek defense with an extensive grove (in ancient times it was still heavily wooded). There is evidence of a wall on the site, though it is not extensive. Taken as a whole, the position provided excellent protection against cavalry and was "...easily defensible against infantry."

As the Persian advance guard moved cautiously inland, to their left and right would be swampy ground which protected their flank. To their front, the ground was relatively flat and as they advanced, the cliffs of the hills overlooking the bay closed in. The Persian advance guard would have to gain the chokepoint formed by the ground where it was funneled by the hills on both sides of the small plain overlooking the bay.

Miltiades had fought with the Persians and he knew their battle tactics. He also knew that his phalanx was vulnerable to the Persian cavalry which would outflank his smaller force with speed and then maneuver into a position where it could pour killing arrows into his men from the flank and rear or even charge them outright. The battle of Ephesus, only eight

© Istituto Archeologico Germanico neg. 61.1192

One of Artaphernes' cavalrymen may be shown on this cup. Once in the Faina Collection in Orvieto (Italy), where it was found. The letters omicron and rho of an inscription can just be made out painted above the left upper arm of the rider.

years earlier, provided an eloquent example of what might happen.

But despite the advantage of his position, despite the strength of the phalanx as a defensive formation and despite knowing that the Persian army would not be able to 'sit them out', the Greek army charged across the plain. Miltiades took a great risk, and won. ●

Ronald Ruiters is a senior Intelligence Officer currently in the Canadian army. He recently returned from a tour at Nato HQ in Brussels. He holds a Masters degree in War Studies and will study Ancient History now that he is back in Canada.

Further reading
- B. Hughes, *Helen of Troy*. New York 2005.
- J. Lacey, *First Clash*. New York 2011.
- T. Holland, *Persian Fire: The First World Empire and the Battle for the West*. London 2005.

Comparing recent reconstructions

How did the battle of Marathon go down?

How did the Athenians win the battle of Marathon? How did a city-state with 30,000 male citizens defeat an invading force sent by a king who ruled 70,000,000 people? Three new books about the battle try to answer this question. Richard Billows, a professor of history at Columbia University, wrote the first; I wrote the second; Jim Lacey, a combat veteran who teaches at the Marine War College and in the Johns Hopkins National Security Program, wrote the third.

By Peter Krentz

We all agree that the earliest account of the battle, written by the Greek historian Herodotus, is by far the best account we have. "The source upon whom we are overwhelmingly dependent for what we know", writes Billows, "is Herodotos." But although Lacey says that Herodotus' "account of the battle is remarkably accurate," modern historians have found numerous faults with his story. As A. W. Gomme once remarked, "Everyone knows that Herodotos' narrative of Marathon will not do." He was not an eyewitness; he talked to (Greek) veterans of the battle, beginning thirty or forty years later. What questions does his account raise?

1. Herodotus does not tell us how many Greeks fought against how many Persians. On the Greek side, he gives a figure only for the 2,000 Spartans who arrived after it was all over (6.120). On the Persian side, he says only that the Persians had 600 triremes (6.95.2). Later sources say 10,000 Athenians and Plataeans faced as many as half a million Persians. What numbers are credible?

2. Herodotus says that the Greeks camped at the sanctuary of Herakles (6.108.1), but he does not locate it clearly. Where was the Greek camp?

3. Herodotus gives Miltiades the leading role among the ten Athenian generals. He says that when the ten generals were divided about whether to risk a battle, Miltiades persuaded the *polemarch*, Kallimachos, "who had been selected by lot," to break the tie by voting in favor of fighting (6.109.2). The command rotated daily, and on his day Miltiades deployed the Athenians for battle (6.111.1). Critics have accused Herodotus of an anachronism, because the Aristotelian *Constitution of Athens* says that the polemarch was the leader of the whole army and that he was elected until 487, three years after Marathon. Who was in command?

4. Herodotus does not say exactly where the fighting took place or give the position of the battle lines clearly. Where did the fighting occur?

5. In Herodotus, Miltiades makes a persuasive speech that the Athenians should fight in order to become the leading city in Greece and to avoid disunity that might lead some to go over to the Persians (6.109.3-6). (The siege of Eretria ended when some citizens betrayed the city and opened the gates.) With Spartans on the way to help, though, why would the Greeks risk advancing into the plain before these allies arrived?

6. Herodotus says that the Persian king Darius had horse-transport ships built the year before (6.95.1), that the Persians put

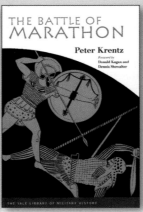

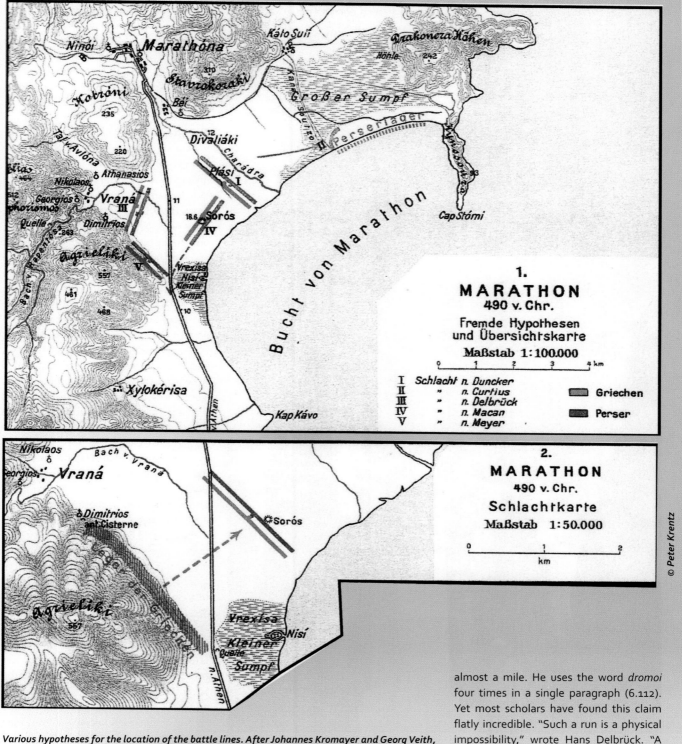

Various hypotheses for the location of the battle lines. After Johannes Kromayer and Georg Veith, *Schlachten-atlas zur* antiken Kriegsgeschichte *(Leipzig 1922) map 1*

almost a mile. He uses the word *dromoi* four times in a single paragraph (6.112). Yet most scholars have found this claim flatly incredible. "Such a run is a physical impossibility," wrote Hans Delbrück. "A heavily equipped unit can cover at the most 400 or 500 feet (120 to 150 meters) at a run without completely exhausting its strength and falling into disorder." Did the Athenians run?

8. Herodotus does not say explicitly how the Greeks won. He describes Miltiades as deploying his men deeper on the wings than in the center (6.111.3). When the Greeks routed the enemy wings but gave

their horses on board at the start of the campaign (6.95.2), and that the Persians landed at Marathon because it "was the region of Attica most suitable for cavalry as well as the one closest to Eretria" (6.102), but then the cavalry disappears from the story. Where was the cavalry during the battle?

7. Herodotus says that the Greeks charged "at a run" (*dromoi*) for eight *stadia*, eight lengths of a Greek stadium, or

The author standing next to the replica of the marble trophy at Marathon.

ground in the center, the Greek wings regrouped and turned against the Persian center (6.113.1-2). Was this a brilliant tactical maneuver planned in advance? Did it determine the outcome of the battle?

Here I propose to review how Billows, Lacey and I answer these questions.

Numbers

We agree that patriotic fervor led the later sources to magnify the victory by minimizing Greek numbers and exaggerating the Persian. Billows puts the Greeks at more than 15,000 Athenians (over 9,000 of them hoplites, the rest light infantry), plus about 600 Plataean hoplites, against about 25,000 Persian infantry and several thousand cavalry, so that the Greeks were outnumbered "perhaps as much as two to one."

Lacey believes in 9,000 Athenian hoplites (he attributes this figure, wrongly, to Herodotus), 1,000 Plataean hoplites, and an unspecified number of light-armed Athenians and slaves — a large number, since Lacey believes the Athenians could field a fighting force numerically equal to the Persians, whom he gives 35,000 infantry and 1,000 cavalry.

I base my estimates for the Greeks on what Herodotus says about the battle of Plataea in 479. There the Athenians had 16,000 men, half of them hoplites, while another 2,000 hoplites were serving as marines (9.28.6, 29.2). So I imagine at least 18,000 Athenians at Marathon, and perhaps as many as 22,000, if we add the 4,000 Athenian settlers who returned from Chalcis just before the battle (6.100.1, assuming that they returned to Chalcis after the Athenian victory). Add about 1,000 Plataeans, about half of them hoplites, for the Plataeans had 600 hoplites and 600 lightly armed troops at the battle fought in their own territory in 479 (6.28.6, 29.2).

We do not really know how many men 600 Persian triremes carried. For Xerxes' fleet in 480, Herodotus assumes 200 men per ship, to which he adds thirty Persians, Medes, or Sakai (7.184.2). If we guess that the regular crew included ten marines (the Athenian standard), Herodotus seems to be thinking of about forty marines per ship, or 24,000 infantry total. I would give the Persians hundreds rather than thousands of cavalry.

Bottom line: The Persians outnumbered the Greeks, but nothing like 50 : 1.

Billows would make the ratio perhaps 5 : 3 or even 2 : 1, while Lacey and I imagine something closer to even, at most 3 : 2.

Where was the Greek camp?
Billows puts the camp "in the hills at the southern end of the plain," near the chapel of Ag. Demetrios. As a result, he favors the battle positions favored by R. W. Macan and N. G. L. Hammond, with the battle lines parallel to the coast (see the map on page 35 for a map showing various older reconstructions of the battle lines; Billows adopts position IV).

Hammond reversed himself after Eugene Vanderpool published two inscriptions from the sanctuary of Herakles, both found in the flat area just north of the narrow southwestern entrance to the plain. Billows ignores Vanderpool's articles. Lacey, on the other hand, says that Vanderpool has "definitely located" the sanctuary. Since the stones were not found in situ, the location is less definite than Lacey believes. But on current evidence, it's the most likely spot. The Greek camp blocked the coast road to Athens. When the Greeks deployed into the plain from this position, they would have lined up more or less perpendicular to the coast.

Who was in command?
Billows sees Kallimachos, the *polemarch*, as the Athenian commander, assisted by the ten generals the Athenians began electing annually in 501/0. Since "all sources agree on giving Miltiades the credit," he believes that Kallimachos allowed Miltiades to determine the battle tactics.

Lacey argues that "the clever old soldier" Kallimachos masterminded the Athenian victory, only to be eclipsed after his death by Miltiades, whose son Kimon successfully promoted his father as the real hero. It is possible, though not demonstrable, that Lacey is correct and that the *polemarch* was the real commander at Marathon. A victory column mentioning Kallimachos was erected on the Acropolis soon after the battle, while the monuments to Miltiades were not put up until the 460s. But Lacey goes on to invent an impossible career for Kallimachos. Lacey's Kallimachos was a military genius who led the Athenians in victories over the Boeotians, the Chalcidians, and the combined forces of the Aeginetans and Argives, over a period of fifteen years.

Arrowheads in the *Soros*
Hammond argued that the arrowheads found in the burial mound show that it was constructed from the earth on which Persian arrows fell, locating the battle at the site of the mound. But the two excavators of the mound, first Heinrich Schliemann and then Valerios Staes, found no arrowheads. The flint 'arrowheads' found by earlier diggers — I do not say archaeologists — turned out to be parts of modern threshing sleds. The bronze arrowheads said to be from Marathon that are now in museums in London and Karlsruhe look like Persian arrowheads, but they have no secure provenience.

Arrowheads said to come from Marathon, now in the British Museum, London.

There is no evidence for any of this, and in fact Kallimachos cannot have commanded at all these battles, since an Athenian was only *polemarch* once, for a single year.

I prefer to accept Herodotus' account, which gives the *polemarch* only the position of honor on the right and the tie-breaking vote when the ten generals were deadlocked. The *Constitution of Athens*, written a hundred years after Herodotus, contains other errors and should not be preferred. Ernst Badian suggested a tempting compromise: The nine *archons* were elected and then a lottery determined which *archon* got which job, so that Kallimachos was both elected and chosen by lot. Though we don't know the details of Miltiades' previous career, he had played a leadership role in the Chersonnese for more than twenty years, so much so that he was charged with tyranny. It isn't much of a leap to think that Miltiades had experience as a military commander.

Where did the fighting occur?
Though Billows' sketchy battle plans do not show the Athenian burial mound known as the *Soros* ("heap"), the caption for his photograph of it makes clear that he believes it marks the site of the battle,

as most historians have supposed.

Lacey's understanding of the topography is more difficult to figure out, since he gives not only no plan of the battle, but also no map of the plain. A caption for his picture of the *Soros* says that "the mound was erected soon after the battle on the location where most of the Athenians fell."

Neither Billows nor Lacey takes into account Vanderpool's discovery of remains of the great marble column that once stood as a trophy for the victory. In 1966, Vanderpool found column drums and an Ionic capital built into a medieval tower adjacent to the chapel of Panagia Mesosporitissa in the middle of the plain, nearly two miles from the *Soros*. In 2004, Nick Sekunda pointed out the critical significance of this find: A Greek trophy — the word derives from the Greek verb for "turn" — marked the spot where the enemy turned and ran. Here, then, is where the two armies met, well out into the plain. A full-size replica in marble now marks the spot (see Figure 2).

Why did the Greeks advancing into the plain? Where was the cavalry?
The conclusion that the two armies met

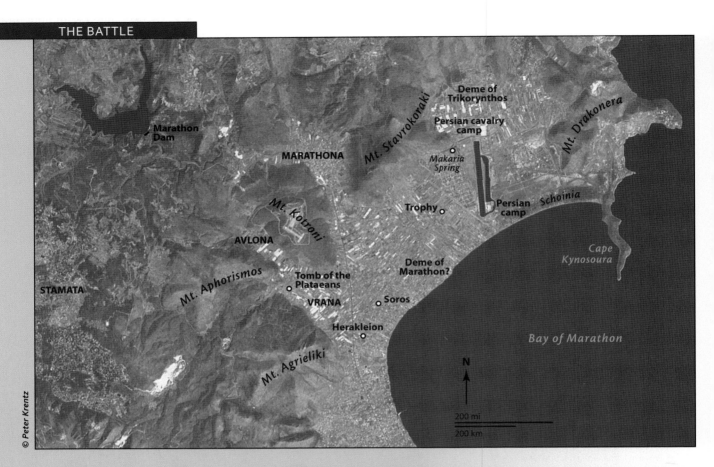

© Peter Krentz

Landsat image of the plain of Marathon, showing the locations of the Herakleion, the Soros, the trophy, and the spring Makaria. When Pausanias visited in the second century AD, the area between the spring and Mt. Drakonera was a marshy lake open to the sea. According to geologist Richard Dunn, it might have accessible for triremes in 490.

at the site of the trophy makes these questions all the more pressing, for it means that the Greeks advanced across the widest part of a plain picked by the Persians because it was so good for cavalry. The Greeks went exactly where one would have thought the Persians wanted to fight, where their superior cavalry could take advantage of the open space. Why would the Greeks have taken such a risk?

Billows and Lacey conclude that they didn't. They follow an idea proposed by a German historian, Ernst Curtius, in the mid-nineteenth century and popularized by an Oxford historian, J. A. R. Munro, in an 1899 article. The idea is that the Persians decided to reembark some of their forces, including their cavalry, and make a dash to Athens. Though this idea rests on what historian Charles Hignett called "no evidence worthy of the name", it has proved remarkably resilient. It's what you see on the History Channel.

Billows and Lacey propose different variations on the theme. Billows suggests that the Persians ships set out at dawn and reached Athens in about twelve hours. The Greeks seized the opportunity to fight on more even terms with the Persians left at

Marathon, won the battle, and returned to Athens as fast as they could, perhaps in seven hours, in time to arrive before the Persian fleet.

Lacey believes that "it is certain that cavalry was present during the battle." He argues that the Persians had not yet finished loading their horses when the fighting started. The Persian horsemen rushed to organize the remaining horses, but they fought only on the beach.

Both scenarios fit some of the evidence. For his race to Athens, Billows can cite Herodotus, who says that "while the Persians were sailing around Sounion, the Athenians were marching back as fast as they could to defend their city, and they managed to arrive there in advance of the barbarian fleet" (6.116). For Persian cavalry fighting on the beach, Lacey can cite a frieze from the Athena Nike temple and a Roman sarcophagus in Brescia, which may be copies of of the great painting of the battle from the 460s, now lost, that once covered a wall in the Stoa Poikile in Athens. "Both depict a vicious fight near the Persian ships," he says, "in which cavalry is clearly present."

Both scenarios also have problems.

While a fit, youthful N. G. L. Hammond once walked from Athens to Marathon in six hours and back in seven, all on the same day, it's difficult to believe that a battle-weary army, starting from the other end of the plain, could have managed the same speed. Nor is it likely that Persian horse-transports averaged five knots for seventy miles from Marathon around Cape Sounion and up to Athens. More probably, as J. T. Hodge has shown, the journey took twenty-four hours and the Athenians hustled back to the city on the day after the battle.

Lacey has a better case. The Brescia sarcophagus does look like a representation of Marathon, since a barbarian is about to chop off the hand of a dying Greek grasping the stern of a ship, recalling how Aeschylus' brother Kynegeiros died (Herodotus 6.114). The sarcophagus shows one horse and one ship. The Nike temple frieze is less securely tied to Marathon. It shows more horses, but no ships. As for Pausanias' description of the painting, which Pausanias saw, it doesn't mention horses at all (1.15.3). So it's less than certain that Persian horses were on the beach.

The biggest difficulty for the cavalry-on-the-ships hypothesis is that no source says the Persians reloaded their horses. There is only an obscure passage in a Byzantine encyclopedia known as the *Suda*, listed under *choris hippeis* ("the cavalry are apart"). J. A. S. Evans' translation indicates different possibilities where the meaning is not clear:

"When Datis invaded Attica, men say that the Ionians, when he had withdrawn [or gone away], came up inland to a wooded area [or climbed trees] and told [or signaled] the Athenians that their horses were apart [or away or brigaded by themselves, or possibly off on a separate mission]. And Miltiades, who took note of their departure [or understood what they were up to], attacked and won a victory."

This passage, written 1500 years after the battle — closer in time to us than to Miltiades — does not cite a source, does not say clearly where the horses were or what they were doing, does not mention ships, and does not explain why the Athenians would need to hear anything from the Ionians. With hills all around, the Marathon plain offers ready visibility. The Athenians ought to have seen for themselves where the horses were.

The Suda is *really* bad evidence. No reconstruction of the battle should rest on it. It sounds to me like a story invented by Ionian Greeks to put a better light on the fact that they were part of the invading force.

If the Persian horses were not on the ships, where were they? The topography of the plain offers a clue. Thirsty horses need water. In the summer of 490, local streams were probably dry, and the marshy lake in the northeastern part of the plain was open to the sea and probably too salty (it may even have been still deep enough for ships). The obvious water source was Makaria, a powerful spring that supplied water to Athens as recently as World War II (the Germans protected it with the round pillbox still visible today). Makaria sits at the northwest corner of what Pausanias describes as a marshy lake (now drained), just below the road that once connected the main plain of Marathon to the smaller plain of Trikorynthos, north of the lake and adjacent to the spring. This smaller plain was, as Colonel William Leake suggested two centuries ago, a likely choice for the

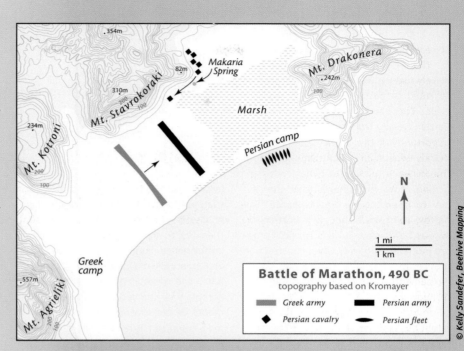

Figure 4: Reconstruction of the battle based on the modern shoreline in Kromayer's map.

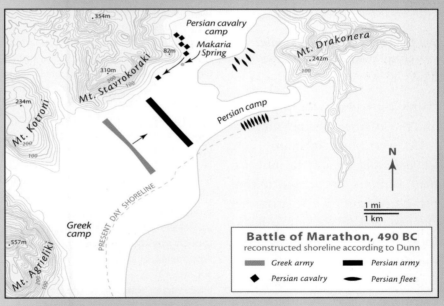

Figure 5: Reconstruction of the battle based on Richard Dunn's reconstruction of the ancient shoreline

cavalry camp. (See Figure 3 for an image of the plain, with the critical locations marked.)

Early nineteenth-century travelers commented on the road between Marathon and Trikorynthos, which passes between Mt. Stavrokoráki and the marsh. Leake reported "traces of ancient wheels" on the rocks in the pass, which Rev. E. D. Clarke described as "hardly wide enough to admit of two persons abreast of each other." At the end of the century,

J. G. Frazer found it only slightly broader, "hardly wide enough for two horses to pass each other."

This topography offers another possible answer to the puzzle of why the Greeks dared to cross the plain. They had several days to watch the Persians deploy. Perhaps the Persians got a little sloppy when the Greeks resisted their challenge to battle. They slept in a bit. They took their positions more slowly. When they heard that the Spartans were on the march, they relaxed a bit more, expecting no real action until the Spartans arrived.

Then — you'll recognize that I'm completely making this up — Miltiades figured he could get inside the enemy's decision cycle. The narrow road separating the Persian cavalry from the plain offered the opportunity. If the Greeks could advance quickly enough and get far enough before the Persians recognized what was happening, it would be too late for the cavalry to intercept the Greek charge. The narrow road would act as a bottleneck. Just as traffic slows to a crawl on a modern interstate highway when construction reduces multiple lanes to one lane, so the Persian horses would have to go single file through the pass to the Marathon plain.

In other words, the Persian horsemen might have missed the battle not because they were on the ships, but because they couldn't get to the Greeks before the hand-to-hand fighting started, after which there was not much they could do.

Did the Greeks run eight *stadia*?
It's worth quoting the critical passage from Herodotus (6.112):

"After the troops were in position and the sacrifices had proven favorable, when the Athenians were let loose and allowed to advance, they charged at a run toward the barbarians. There were not fewer than eight stadia (0.9 miles) between the two armies. When the Persians saw the Athenians running toward them, they were preparing to meet the attack; they assumed that the Athenians were seized by some utterly self-destructive madness, as they observed how few the Athenians were in number and how they were running toward them with neither cavalry nor archers in support. So the barbarians suspected that the Athenians had gone mad, but when the Athenians closed all together [athrooi] with them in combat, they fought remarkably well. For they were the first of all Greeks we

know of to use the running charge against their enemies, as well as the first to endure the sight of the Medes' clothing and the men wearing it. In fact, until then, even to hear the name 'Medes' spoken would strike terror into Greeks."

In the 1970s, Walter Donlan and Thompson tried to test this account by giving college students some weight to carry, hooking them up to various devices in a human performance laboratory, having them run on a treadmill at a pace of seven miles per hour, and measuring the results. Billows accepts their conclusion that these experiments demonstrated that heavily-armed men could not have run more than 150 meters without becoming too exhausted to fight. Billows also argues that the range of Persian archers meant that the Greeks had no need to run farther than 150 meters, or even 100 meters. In his reconstruction, Greeks carrying sixty pounds or more ran only when arrows began to fall. Herodotus apparently exaggerates.

Based partly on his experience interviewing Iraq war veterans eighteen months after the event — and comparing those interviews to transcripts of interviews given only a few days after the fall of Baghdad — Lacey objects that adrenalin produces clear battlefield memories of events men participate in directly. He argues that the Donlan-Thompson tests are invalid because the college students, though physical education majors, were not trained in carrying heavy loads. He concedes that a mile sprint would have wrecked the cohesion of the phalanx, so he concludes that they advanced double time for most of the distance, beginning a "real run" only when they came within range of the Persian archers. Lacey does not explain why the Greeks advanced rapidly before they came within bowshot.

To my mind, this issue of the running charge is *the* critical issue, because it is what Herodotus emphasizes. For Herodotus, the running charge was the key to the battle. Is his story credible?

First, the issue of weight. Perhaps the most important general thesis in my book concerns the weight of hoplite equipment. The oft-quoted figure of 72 pounds goes back to an 1852 German book in which the authors simply estimated what vari-

ous items weighed. I will not go into the details here, but finds of ancient equipment and reconstructions made by reenactors now permit evidence-based numbers. An Athenian hoplite in 490 carried 28-45 lbs, or even less if he did without a corselet and shin guards.

Second, the issue of speed. People switch from a walking gait to running — that is, there's at least a moment when neither foot touches the ground — at about 4.5 miles per hour. Five miles per hour, or twelve minutes a mile, would certainly satisfy what Herodotus says; seven miles per hour, much less a full sprint, is unnecessary.

Third, the issue of phalanx cohesion. Again I will not go into the details here, but I am not one of the literalists who maintain that hoplites fought with shields overlapping or even touching. Certainly there is nothing in Herodotus that requires such tight cohesion. The word *athrooi*, which the standard Greek-English dictionary translates "in close order," means nothing more than "all together." In a good parallel, the poet Pindar has the leaders of the Cadmeans run *athrooi* in their bronze armor into the infant Herakles' bedroom (*Nemean* 1.51). Pindar must mean "all together" or "all at once" rather than "in close order." Or take the historian Thucydides' account of the Plataeans, escaping from their besieged city on a dark and stormy night: they proceeded *athrooi* along the road to Thebes (3.24.1). They were not marching in the rain with interlocked shields as they fled from their enemies.

When I asked former Davidson College ROTC graduates about their experiences running with weight, many described jogging with a 35-pound rucksack and a heavy rifle for multiple miles. Their experiences are consistent with what Jim Lacey describes. Like Lacey, I have no doubt that what Herodotus says here is believable.

Should we believe him? "Possibility," objects Billows, "is really beside the point: it would have made no sense to do it. Why should the Athenians exhaust themselves running hundreds of meters ... when Persian bows were only effective at around 150 meters?"

Why, indeed? My suggestion: Miltiades didn't time the advance quite right. When the Greeks were still about a mile from the enemy, someone saw Persian horses entering the plain. Knowing that they had to cross the widest part of the plain before the cavalry arrived, Miltiades yelled and the men began to jog. Persian arrows, which Herodotus does not mention at Marathon, had nothing to do with the Athenian run; Persian horses, which he does mention, had everything to do with it. The run prevented the cavalry from outflanking the hoplites and interrupting the Greek charge. (See figures 4 and 5.)

How did the Greeks win?

We three agree that the Persian horsemen did not affect the outcome, that the Greeks successfully ran through the storm of Persian arrows, and that the desperate Greeks, fighting in defense of their land, had better armor and weapons for a hand-to-hand battle. We differ on the extent to which Greek commanders anticipated exactly how the struggle would go.

Billows maintains that Miltiades "developed a uniquely innovative and complex plan of battle." He deployed his men in such a way that his line matched the length of the Persian line, but to do that he thinned his center to (say) only four ranks deep, while the wings were the standard eight deep. The whole line stretched around 1600 meters, or about a mile. The battle went as Miltiades planned. The Greek wings routed their opponents, then stopped and—as Miltiades had ordered before the fighting began—turned to help the center. As the Persians began to realize they were outflanked on both sides, the Persian formation began to melt away, and a desperate flight to the ships began.

Though he credits Kallimachos rather than Miltiades, Lacey also thinks the Greeks had a "novel" and "brilliant" plan; his reconstruction is virtually identical to Billows'. Lacey stresses how impressive the Greeks' performance was: the slow, deliberate withdrawal of the center, without breaking ranks, matched by the halt, reformation, ninety-degree turn and another charge on both flanks. Lacey judges these actions "impossible," except for a "professional force as part of a preset plan." An army veteran himself, Lacey really wants the credit for Marathon to go to a disciplined, professional army led by a brilliant, seasoned general (recall that he invented an impressive resumé for Kallimachos).

But is it credible that the Athenians had a professional army in 490? On the basis of a victory against the Thebans

in 519, a willingness to take the field against the Peloponnesians in 506, victories against the Thebans and then the Chalcidians in 506, followed by another victory against the Thebans and then against the Aeginetans and Argives, Lacey argues that "the Athenians were a highly professional and well-disciplined force," and even, in these years, "just as much a nation in arms as Sparta." Not only is this argument weak in itself (five wins in almost thirty years against amateur armies do not prove that the Athenians were a professional force), but the Athenians, unlike the Spartans, had no helots to work their land, freeing them to be professional soldiers. And not only that, but we have explicit literary evidence that the Athenians did not train together. Thucydides quotes Pericles as bragging that the Athenians are just as brave as their enemies without subjecting themselves to the rigorous training Spartans undergo (2.39.1), and Xenophon quotes Socrates as saying that the Athenians have no public military training (*Memorabilia* 3.12.5).

I agree with Lacey that an army of amateurs could not have carried out such a plan. But Herodotus does not require anything so complicated. He says that the result of the Athenians' deployment was a line equal to the Persian formation in length, but only a few rows deep in the center (6.111.3). That formation could have resulted from the simple desire not to be outflanked: The Athenian right hugged the coast, while the Plataeans on the left made sure their line reached Mt. Stavrokoráki. The center stretched as a result. Herodotus also does not require a planned, double-pincer movement. He simply says that when the Greeks routed the Persian wings, they let them go, regrouped, and went to help the center. For all we know, it was standard Greek practice not to pursue too far before making sure the entire battle was won.

In short, if we approach Herodotus with sufficient goodwill, his account makes sense. Herodotus highlights the run for almost a mile. The Greeks could have jogged a mile, and — the topography offers the clue — they might have needed to jog a mile in order to cross the widest part of the plain and close with the Persian infantry before the cavalry could intercept them. Miltiades' plan was a good one: Keep the cavalry out of the battle and minimize the Persian advantage in

infantry numbers by arming every available man with a spear and a shield. (That's why Herodotus says the Persians were amazed to see the Greeks charging without archers or cavalry, 6.112.2, and why he mentions the Greeks were "all together," *athrooi*, 6.112.3.)

Once the Greeks made it through the storm of arrows and hand-to-hand fighting began, the Persian cavalry commander could do little and must have begun to board the ships. Greek hoplite infantry, with sturdier defensive equipment and longer thrusting spears, overcame first the Persian wings and then the Persian center. The Greeks pursued the invaders all the way back to their ships.

Perhaps it is fair to say that Miltiades put the Greeks in a position where they could win. But credit should go above all to the men who elected him, who voted to take the field, who made the unprecedented running charge, and who fought to defend their land, their families, and their freedom.

The ancient biographer Plutarch says that when Miltiades asked the Athenian assembly for the honor of a crown of olive leaves, an Athenian retorted, "When you have fought and defeated the barbarians by yourself, Miltiades, then you may ask to be honored by yourself." ●

Peter Krentz is W. R. Grey Professor of Classics and History at Davidson College in North Carolina. Apart from the book mentioned in this article, he has published extensively about warfare in the Greek world.

Further reading:
- R.A. Billows, *Marathon: How One Battle Changed Western Civilization*. New York 2010.
- P. Krentz, *The Battle of Marathon*. New Haven 2010.
- J. Lacey, *The First Clash: The Miraculous Greek Victory at Marathon and Its Impact on Western Civilization*. New York 2011.

The Greek formation would inevitably have been disordered when it hit the Persian lines. Impetus, better armor and better close-combat weaponry helped the Greeks to carry the day.

© Jason Askew

Battlefield stress in ancient Greek warfare

The blinding of Epizelus

As the fog of war descends upon the battlefield the clatter of armour from nervous fidgeting rises and the drum beating in the chest of every hoplite reverberates throughout his body. The paean is struck up, goose bumps shudder on skin. The adrenaline rush is in full flow, an eye begins to twitch, stomachs begin to turn. Stirrings to evacuate are subdued as the signal is given to advance. With each step the battle draws nearer, the breathing gets heavier, hearts racing within chests. As the clash of weapons erupts through the eardrums, minds go blank, with only flashes of cognition they act as they have been trained. They fight and they kill, their only aim is to survive.

By Owen Rees

And so the fighting descends into an experiential chaos. It is within these stressful parameters that the experience of battle existed, and it is in stress that we can find the universal human element within ancient warfare.

The story of Epizelus
As the study of Marathon rages on, it becomes easier and easier to ignore the individuals fighting reducing them to statistics and elusive manoeuvres. However, Herodotus gives one such individual who scholars have ignored, dismissed or manipulated to conform to their overarching theories. His story is a short one, and on the surface very simple, but Herodotus picks him out of the thousands of individual experiences of the battle due to the unusual nature of what he went through:

"an Athenian, Epizelus son of Couphagoras, was fighting as a brave man in the battle when he was deprived of his sight, though struck or hit nowhere on his body, and from that time on he spent the rest of his life in blindness."

Herodotus, Histories *6.117.2.*

For a man to lose his sight for no external reason is bizarre but not unheard of. What allows us to examine this more thoroughly is the reason Epizelus used to give when telling the story:

"I have heard that he tells this story about his misfortune: he

saw opposing him a tall armed man, whose beard overshadowed his shield, but the phantom passed him by and killed the man next to him."

Herodotus, Histories *6.117.3.*

This story has recently been put to use by authors such a Tritle (2002) who identify this account as an example of psychological trauma on the battlefield. This is what was once known as 'hysterical blindness' and in turn is used as an example of ancient Post Traumatic Stress Disorder (PTSD). The psychosomatic (emotionally induced) nature of this 'diagnosis' is convenient as it is as impossible to disprove as it is to prove. It is based upon the idea that by seeing this one single event, the death of a comrade, the mind could not cope with the information it was receiving and so refuses to see it – hence the blindness.

There is perhaps a more biological explanation, which may also explain why Epizelus never *regained* his sight, something not explained by the short term trauma theory expounded above. But to understand this we have to stop looking at this from modern philosophical underpinnings and engage the Greeks in their own explanations and context.

Part of the marble frieze of Athena Nike ("Victorious Athena") on the Acropolis at Athens, showing heroically nude Greeks fighting mounted Persians. It has been interpreted as the death of the polemarch Callimachus at Marathon, but that interpretation is currently doubted. Now in the British Museum, London.

Physical wounds: this scene has been interpreted as Achilles bandaging the wounds of Patroclus. Note the rare representation of the 'cap-comforter' worn by Patroclus, and how the scales run downwards at the back of the shoulder-guard assembly. The arrow in the shield is possibly a reference to the threat from Persian archers that the Greek hoplites would face in the future. Now in the Altes Museum, Berlin.

The relevance of Pan

One important aspect of the Persian Wars that scholars have been highlighting recently is that the period appears to have been the beginning of the hoplite/phalanx cohesion we see exemplified by the end of the 5th century. This 'tactical reform', if it can be called that, saw in turn a change of attitudes based on new threats. Compared to the heroic fighting ideal we see in Homer, the emphasis became one of unity and structure. If a man left the lines he put the entire formation in jeopardy, something the Spartan Aristodemus ignored at Plataea and so he did not receive any honours (9.71.3-4).

This raised a new problem for the soldiers, something that had been seen but had no real impact in earlier warfare: the devastating effect of panic on the formation. If only a few men panicked, it put the lives of everyone else in danger. This may seem more like conjecture, and perhaps we are over-emphasising the change in attitudes as military ideas evolved, but it is perhaps more than a little interesting that it is just before Marathon that Herodotus re-introduces the god Pan into

his narrative and that it is after Marathon that the cult of Pan is meant to have been established within Athens.

"When [Pheidippides] was in the Parthenian mountain above Tegea he encountered Pan. Pan called out Pheidippides' name and bade him ask the Athenians why they paid him no attention, though he was of goodwill to the Athenians, had often been of service to them, and would be in the future. The Athenians believed that these things were true, and when they became prosperous they established a sacred precinct of Pan beneath the Acropolis"

Herodotus, Histories 6.105.1-3.

What we have in Herodotus' notoriously unreliable account is a connection with not just hearsay but also worship and ritual.

No matter what can be questioned about this account, the Athenians did include Pan into the pantheon of the Acropolis around this time and it seems unlikely that Herodotus was lying about the sacrifice and races held in his honour every year. The tradition of Pan's impact on Marathon can be seen in the supposed epigram of Miltiades in his dedication to the God;

"I, Goat-footed Pan, the Arkadian, enemy of the Medes, ally of the Athenians, was set up by Miltiades."

Simonides fragment V.

The reason for this newly found devotion comes from the impact Pan had on all living things, his ability to induce panic (a concept duly named after him). This ability was supposedly evident from the moment he was born:

"And in the house she bare Hermes a dear son who from his birth was marvellous to look upon, with goat's feet and two horns —a noisy, merry-laughing child. But when the nurse saw his uncouth face and full beard, she was afraid and sprang up and fled and left the child."

Hymn to Pan, 35-40.

This personification of a human experience is not unusual within Greek mythology and seems to show a desire to explain the unexplainable. From his arrival on the Greek military stage in Herodotus, Pan's influence can be seen right through to the end of the classical period both explicitly and implicitly within the texts of writers such as Thucydides and Xenophon.

But what has this to do with Epizelus, and what has this to do with the impact of stress in Greek warfare?

Modern models

Panic, as the Greeks explained it, mostly incorporated fear and the act of running away, something the Persians were prone to within Herodotus' and Xenophon's narratives, no doubt helping the reputation of Pan as being an enemy of the Persians. However, modern studies into 'panic' (stress reactions) have produced further repercussive actions which, when combined with running away, created the 'Fight – Flight – Freeze' syndrome. But even this model simplifies what is a very complex biological reaction to stress, especially combat or survival stress.

Within ancient historical study a thread has appeared since Keegan's (non-ancient history) book, *The Face of Battle*, which built upon a desire to know more about the individual experiences of battle rather than the larger scaled tactics and leading personalities. This progressed through Victor Hanson's work into the newest manifestations led by psychoanalyst Jonathan Shay, and classicist Lawrence Tritle. This has directed our attentions away from the experience of combat and into the impact of trauma on the returning veterans. This avenue of study has been dominated by psychoanalytical theory and gaps have been filled with modern therapy notes. This school of thought takes for granted that all war is traumatic, that all trauma is pretty much the same and so manifests in the same way; hence Epizelus being diagnosed with hysterical blindness. Its emphasis is on the mind rather than the body. However, new research is allowing us to bypass so much theory and conjecture and return to the issue of causation. Rather than focus on the possible outcome, trauma, we can begin at the beginning: combat stress.

It would be easy for this to descend into a biology paper, which, although valid, does not make for interesting reading. The important aspects for us to understand are threefold:

(1) What caused the stress reaction is important to understand what reaction happened (think of the difference between the flinch reactions from touching a hot pot, to the tears that occur with the news of a lost loved one).

(2) The brain regions most associated with stress reactions, such as the Amygdala, are present in all mammals and serve the same functions within stress (i.e. this is a universal human biological experience).

(3) How stress manifests itself, is subject to a plethora of factors from upbringing, education, social parameters, personality, context, age, gender and so forth, but the biology remains the same. In other

words, if you induce stress in someone we can (pretty much) guarantee a high level of epinephrine (adrenaline). How this affects behaviour cannot be predicted as easily. It may not be apparent in some people, cause only a twitch in the eye in others, while it may leave again others physically shaking. These aspects combined allow us to look at the effects of these hormones in the short and long term, allowing us to decode behaviour reported by our sources within a more likely biological context.

Because of our understanding of the biology we can begin to fill in gaps left by the sources due to lack of interest, understanding or even social taboos. Adrenaline is commonly understood by most so we have no need to dwell there (but it has allowed us to paint an accurate picture of experience when it may be thought we are using poetic licence, such as the opening paragraph above). Cortisol is another important hormone, which flows throughout your body whilst it is under combat / survival stress. It is a hormonal steroid, which, among many other things, suppresses the immune system and has inflammatory qualities. It has been used to explain feats of super-human activity such as the ability to run with a broken leg. More simply it explains why things don't hurt whilst in the stress reaction as much as they do once it has subsided. Cortisol is important to historians to understand as it can prevent us from ignoring stories within our sources, such as Epizelus as we shall explore later, and also links us to the psychoanalytical school of studying trauma.

Although the full biology of PTSD is not yet understood, it has been proven that the presence of cortisol within chronic stress is the cause of many of the symptoms associated with the disorder, including the destruction of grey matter. By understanding the biology of stress we have reached the same conclusions as Shay and Tritle, but from a much stronger methodological basis and based upon many fewer assumptions.

Phobos

As we return to ancient Greek constructs we must also look to the cause of panic (other than Pan, obviously) that is so often cited by the sources – *Phobos*, fear. It is where we inherited the term phobia, and the fear it describes is interestingly attributed to both animals and humans,

implying once again a universality to the experience.

Fear takes many forms, much like stress, and the two concepts overlap in so many ways that they can even seem inseparable in some contexts, but separate they are. If the fear of something is from an imminent stimulus, then the biological reaction is that of survival stress. However if the fear exists in a future event, it is not the same. This cognitive stress (stress induced by thoughts rather than external factors) is the cause of chronic stress or, in other words, prolonged stress. For instance, the fear of battle a week before it happens, starts a stress reaction which lasts the entire week and is then accentuated as combat stress reactions occur. The presence of fear gives us the needed evidence of prolonged stress, increasing the likelihood of neurological damage/trauma.

For the Greeks at Marathon the most obvious fear, as with all humans, was the unknown. In this case the Persians. How do we know the Greeks afraid of the Persians, you may ask? Well, Herodotus gives us a concise description:

"[The Greeks at Marathon] are also the first to endure looking at Median dress and men wearing it, for up until then just hearing the name of the Medes caused the Hellenes to panic."

Herodotus, Histories 6.112.3.

These were the first Athenians to properly face a Persian force, an army they had heard much about and had taken control of the largest empire their world had seen. They were a foreign people the Greeks could not understand. They were not 'savage' nomadic tribes like those to the north, but neither were they Greek in any respect.

Another fear seldom dwelled upon is that of the hoplite for their family or friend's welfare. This may sound rather

Epizelus' moment of crisis. Probably filled with worry since news of the Persian invasion, survival stress from the battle itself has raised his body's cortisol to a dangerous and damaging level.

An earlier type of Corinthian helmet showing battle damage. A sword or axe crashed smashed right through the bowl. Now in the Allard Pierson Museum, Amsterdam, the Netherlands.

© Karwansaray Publishers

soppy, even anachronistic, but we have evidence from other encounters about these concerns. Most notably it can be found in our only first-hand source of an army of Greeks on campaign: Xenophon's *Anabasis* (admittedly coming 90 years later). During a moment of great despair the soldiers are described as such,

"Many did not come that night to their quarters, but lay down wherever they each chanced to be, unable to sleep for grief and longing for their native states and parents, their wives and children, whom they thought they should never see again. Such was the state of mind in which they all lay down to rest."

Xenophon, *Anabasis* 3.1.3.

We get similar comments in Lysias and Thucydides as well, allowing us to see a shimmering glimpse of emotional reality for the hoplite, behind the veneer of macho pride. So, although Herodotus does not share this emotional torment with us, maybe because it was not shared with him (the macho pride was as much an obstacle for him as it is for us now), it is not unreasonable to include this within the remit of future fears felt by some if

not many.

This form of stress creates a similar, but slower, biological reaction to combat stress and so our old friend cortisol is found in very high levels to people suffering with what is known as 'chronic stress'. Constantly high levels of this hormone are dangerous and have large adverse effects, from something as simple as being regularly ill (due to the suppression of the immune system) to results as damaging as memory loss (due to the killing of particular brain cells).

Returning to Epizelus

As we draw back from this methodological minefield and return to our hero in question we can re-examine the event once more, with a better understanding of context as well as the repercussions to said context.

We know little about Epizelus the man, his thoughts, his emotions and his views. However, if we assume him to be an 'average' hoplite for the period, we can begin to piece his story together. He would have been inexperienced in combat, having *at most* fought in one or two small battles before Marathon. He would not have really encountered a Persian, especially in combat, and so would have feared them and their alien ways. This fear will have been fuelled by Athenian propaganda as well as rumours. It will have grown with the first sight of them and the fear of the unknown becomes a fear of the imminent. He would have had concerns for the future of his city and even his family. As battle began and the adrenaline was pumping he would have had extra shots of it with each new stimulus such as the positive omens being read, the order to advance, the order to run and the melee itself.

He would have had high levels of cortisol running throughout his body in the battle, if not the days leading up due to his fear, due to his cognitive stress. As he fought he saw the man next to him (possibly a friend or at least an acquaintance) killed, at which moment he became blind – never to see again. When asked later he told of a giant phantom figure, most likely the man who killed his brother in arms in a mythologised perception.

This blindness can be explained, not so much by the final stimulus of the killing, but by the presence of cortisol. Where some historians have diagnosed a psychosomatic 'hysterical blindness', the bio-

logical equivalent is called 'central serous retinopathy.' This is blindness caused by a leakage within the eye and subsequent swelling, caused by a weakening of the capillaries at the back of the eye, which in turn is commonly caused by either steroids or . . . high exposure to cortisol. Although blindness is not usually permanent under this diagnosis, a permanent reduction in sight is not uncommon which raises the question how blind did an ancient Greek have to be to claim he was? So although this appears to be a similar conclusion to the psychoanalytical theory, it is more encompassing of the full experience that Epizelus would have had rather than just the singular traumatic event in isolation.

To really understand Greek warfare, the experience of combat on an individual level needs to be explored. This means starting at the beginning, pointing out many obvious factors and exploring areas of study not usually included within the historians remit. Epizelus is just one story of many from the Ancient Greek narrative, and is one that can help bridge the missing link in our knowledge of warfare – what was it like?

As easy, and enjoyable, as it is to look at the formation of battle and the tactical ingenuity involved; we cannot distance ourselves from the realities of warfare and its effects. In ancient Greece, as well as now, war was stressful, it was highly emotional and its impact was lasting, causing traumatic issues ranging from the obscure to the glamorous and even to the mundane. It may not be a pleasant topic, and for some it may be too close to home, but a reality it was and an essential element of ancient warfare it must become. ●

Owen Rees is a postgraduate researcher at UCL, specialising in Ancient Greek battlefield trauma and how it was dealt with by civic society. His website is www.owenrees.co.uk

Further reading:
- J. Shay, *Achilles in Vietnam: combat trauma and the undoing of character.* New York 1994.
- J. Shay, *Odysseus in America: Combat Trauma and the Trials of Homecoming.* New York 2003.
- L. Tritle, *From Melos to My Lai: War and Survival.* London 2000.

Why were the Spartans late for Marathon?

Meanwhile, in Sparta

The Greek philosopher Plato thought it disgraceful that only one of the great powers of Greece had taken the field at Marathon to repulse the Persian invaders. Argos, for one, had ignored the Athenians' call to arms, and thus failed to contribute to the defence of Greece. Only the joint determination of Athens and Sparta, by Plato's reckoning, ensured that Greece did not fall under Persian slavery. But it is an inconvenient truth for Plato's argument that Sparta had not actually fought at Marathon, either. Her hoplites had arrived on the day following the battle. So, why were the Spartans late for the Battle of Marathon?

By Duncan B. Campbell

Before the Persian invasion of Greece, Sparta had been ruled, for many years, by the Agiad King Cleomenes, and his Eurypontid counterpart Demaratus. (Sparta was traditionally ruled by a pair of kings, who represented the bloodline of the two royal houses.) The two men did not see eye to eye.

Cleomenes had already participated in the ousting of the tyrant Hippias from Athens (510 BC), but his replacement by the democrat Cleisthenes displeased the Spartan, whose natural affinity was with oligarchic rule. The subsequent full mobilisation of the Spartan army, for the purposes of invading Attica (507 BC), fell apart owing to discord with her Peloponnesian allies; Demaratus sided with the Peloponnesians. It was for this very reason, according to Herodotus, that no two Spartan kings were ever again allowed to take the field together.

Earth and water

Athens had, meanwhile, made abortive overtures to the Persians, but drew the line at granting the required 'earth and water', the tokens of submission to Persian rule. On the other hand, fifteen years later, in 491 BC, when the Persian

king Darius finally conceived his plan to invade Greece, 'earth and water' were willingly given by the island of Aegina, nursing a long-term grievance against her larger neighbour Athens, a grievance encouraged by the Thebans, who were traditionally anti-Athenian.

By contrast, the Athenians, when asked for the same tokens, memorably threw the Persian envoys into a pit like common criminals; the Spartans followed suit, employing a well for the same purpose, while advising the Persians, with their customary laconic wit, that they could find earth and water down there!

In Aegina, Athens feared a pro-Persian enemy in her rear. Sparta clearly saw the danger, too; but Cleomenes' attempt to punish the Aeginetan medizers was, somewhat predictably, blocked by the troublesome Demaratus, whereupon Cleomenes engineered his deposition (assisted by the peculiar Spartan tradition of evaluating their kings every eight years for suitability). Demaratus was replaced by the more like-minded Leotychidas, and the Spartans duly deposited ten Aeginetan hostages at Athens. (Herodotus has the whole story at 6.49-50 and 73.)

Demaratus subsequently took refuge

at the court of the Persian king, thus proving that his loyalties were at odds with Cleomenes' passionately anti-Persian stance. Cleomenes, on the other hand, returned not to Sparta but to Arcadia. As war loomed with Persia, what was Cleomenes up to?

The schemes of Cleomenes

Herodotus – perhaps misled by a source sympathetic to Demaratus' plight, or perhaps simply confused by the notorious Spartan secrecy – believed that Cleomenes now worked against Sparta, fomenting revolt in Arcadia.

"After this, when Cleomenes' treachery against Demaratus became known, he feared the Spartans and went off to Thessaly in secret. Having reached Arcadia from there, he plotted a rebellion, uniting the Arcadians against Sparta, making them swear oaths to follow him wherever he led; and zealously brought the leading men of the Arcadians to the city of Nonacris to swear by the water of the River Styx."

Herodotus, Histories 6.74.1

This interpretation of Cleomenes' actions seems unlikely. On the other hand, Herodotus is no doubt right when he claims that the Spartan king made the Arcadian leaders swear their holiest oaths that they would follow his lead. For, having ensured that Athens had no enemy in her rear, Cleomenes was surely now bolstering Sparta against potential waverers and medizers.

Indeed, Cleomenes' visit to Arcadia was supposedly preceded by a visit to Thessaly, which scholars have found inexplicable. One solution has been to emend

"Thessalia" in Herodotus' Greek to read "Sellasia", a town to the north of Sparta which is at least broadly in the neighbourhood of Arcadia. However, if Cleomenes was really assembling allies against the Persian threat, Thessaly may have been an appropriate destination; her communities would be required to stand firm as a counterbalance to anti-Athenian Thebes, while supporting their pro-Athenian neighbours on Euboea, an avowed Persian target.

Wherever Thessaly fits into the puzzle, at this stage, Herodotus presents the curious story of Cleomenes' madness and death. His evidence, that the king took to brandishing his wooden staff in the faces of fellow Spartans, may simply be a symptom of Cleomenes' violent and impulsive nature. The king's reported fatal self-mutilation, however, is more difficult to explain away, unless it was a story cooked up by murderers to conceal a regicide, as some scholars have suggested.

Herodotus' narrative is muddled at this point, and it is not clear how the business with the medizing Aeginetans fits chronologically with the unfolding Persian narrative, culminating in the Battle of Marathon. At some stage, Cleomenes' coregent, Leotychidas, was accused of having wronged the Aeginetans, and when he attempted to remedy matters, the Athenians refused to release the hostages to him, saying that two Spartan kings had deposited them, so two Spartan kings must redeem them. The point of the tale is that, because Cleomenes (one of the two depositors) was, by now, dead, the two parties had reached stalemate. But when did he die?

Most scholars have assumed that Herodotus' narrative is strictly chronological, so that the entire Aeginetan affair (recounted at 6.50, 73, and 85-93, interspersed with background material on Sparta and her kings) preceded the Persian expedition (recounted at 6.94-102) and the ensuing Battle of Marathon. But a few dissenters have queried whether the Aeginetan affair could really have reached such an early conclusion. The Oxford historian and veteran Spartan scholar, Antony Andrewes, called it "an intolerable compression." It seems that we cannot simply assume that Cleomenes died before the Battle of Marathon.

The Oath of Marathon

In the summer of 490 BC, as soon as the Athenians heard that the Persians had captured Euboea, they sent out requests for help in all directions. We have seen that Cleomenes had probably been working to counter any medizing, both at Sparta, with the removal of Demaratus, and on Aegina, with the incarceration of hostages at Athens. At the same time, he was assembling an anti-Persian confederation, with his visits to Arcadia and Thessaly; for, in the north, where Thebes could not be counted upon to support Athens, only the little town of Plataea was a staunch Athenian ally.

An interesting inscription from Acharnae (c. 10km north of Athens) preserves a copy of the "oath which the Athenians swore when they were about to fight against the barbarians" (Rhodes and Osborne, *Greek Historical Inscriptions*, no. 88). Most scholars have assumed that this oath was taken on the occasion of Xerxes' invasion (480-479 BC), but it seems more likely that it refers to the Battle of Marathon. While differing from the later oath in certain key respects, the inscription specifically refers to the allies as Athens, Sparta, and Plataea, and promises to preserve these cities "and any other allied town" from destruction while threatening specific punishment upon Thebes. So if Sparta had sworn the oath – indeed, if Cleomenes had been instrumental in organising it – why did the Spartans not fight at Marathon?

The 'official story'

Herodotus explains that, when the Athenian messenger, Pheidippides, arrived in Sparta with news that the Persians had captured Eretria on Euboea, he found that the Spartans were unable to assist.

"*After this, Pheidippides was sent by the generals ... he reached Sparta on the day after he left the city of Athens and, coming to the magistrates, he said, 'Spartans, the Athenians ask you to come to their aid and not look on as the most ancient city of the Greeks falls into slavery at the hands of barbarians; for, even now, Eretria has been reduced to slavery and Greece has become weaker by one important city.' When he announced*

what he had been ordered to say, they agreed to help the Athenians, but it was impossible for them to do so immediately, as they did not wish to break their law, for it was the ninth of the month, and they said that they could not march out on the ninth, not until the circle [i.e. the moon] was full."

Herodotus, Histories *6.106*

Scholars usually assume that the Spartans must have been celebrating a sacred festival, perhaps even the well-known Carneia. However, the topic is fraught with difficulty, not least because of our ignorance of the Dorian calendar used at Sparta. Some scholars have tried to match Herodotus' date ("the ninth of the month") with the incidence of a full moon, but the particular month need not have been critical. Pausanias, for one, believed that "the Spartans had put off marching because they had a law never to march out to battle until the circle of the moon was full" (*Description of Greece* 1.28.4). Of course, religious scruples could be ignored whenever they proved inconvenient, and we are perhaps simply reading Herodotus' rationalisation of an event that he did not understand. For why else would the Spartans have delayed their departure?

Plato's version

Scholars have periodically drawn attention to the alternative explanation offered by Plato.

"*The Athenians were panic-stricken and sent out envoys in all directions but no one was willing to help except the Spartans; but they were hindered by the war going on at that time against Messene, or by something else that we don't know about, so that they arrived one day late for the battle that took place at Marathon.*"

Plato, Laws *3.698e*

It is usual to point out that there is no other evidence of such a "war against

Messene" at that precise time. However, Strabo writes that "the Spartans often went to war on account of the revolts of the Messenians" (*Geography* 8.4.10). The Second Messenian War, celebrated in the poetry of Tyrtaeus, took place around 700 BC, and another, usually called the Third Messenian War, blew up in the aftermath of the great earthquake at Sparta in 465 BC. Yet, having stated that "the second war was in the time of Tyrtaeus", Strabo continues: "but a third and fourth war took place, they say, in which the Messenians were defeated." If our third war, dated to around 465 BC, was really Strabo's fourth war, when did the Third Messenian War really take place?

Pausanias preserves the interesting tale that, at some point, fleeing Messenians assisted Anaxilas of Rhegium to capture the town of Zankle on Sicily, which was renamed Messina in their honour (*Description of Greece* 4.23.6-10). Coin issues from the new town have been dated to 488 BC. So it seems at least possible that the new inhabitants of Zankle were refugees escaping from a Spartan crackdown in Messene, precisely at the time of the Battle of Marathon.

Indeed, there is an echo of such an event in Herodotus' account, which the historian clearly did not fully understand. For, some time before Marathon, when Aristagoras, the tyrant of Miletus, came to Sparta to persuade the kings to invade Persia, he advised Cleomenes to "postpone your fight against the Messenians, who are your equals in battle and whose land is neither so extensive nor fertile and is limited by confining boundaries, and to cease fighting against the Arcadians and Argives, who have no gold or silver" (Herodotus, 5.49.8).

In fact, shortly afterwards, Cleomenes made a pre-emptive strike against the Argives at Sepeia, preventing them from meddling in Spartan affairs (and, indeed, in Persian affairs, if we accept Cleomenes' agenda of protecting Athens' rear against medizing Greeks). Furthermore, as we have seen, Cleomenes went on to secure a diplomatic agreement with the Arcadians, presumably for much the same reasons. That leaves only the Messenians.

How ironic, if, having worked to ensure the protection of Athens, Cleomenes had failed to safeguard his own rear against Messene.

Scenes of hoplites saying goodbye to their loved ones or sacrificing to a deity are commonly seen in figurative painting. This classically equipped hoplite – wearing a Corinthian helmet and likely a yoke-and-tube corselet to protect his torso, has attached a (leather?) apron to his shield for increased protection. Now in the Altes Museum, Berlin.

© Karwansaray Publishers

An alternative version?

Some scholars have asked whether the Spartans really had any intention of joining the Battle of Marathon at all, but Herodotus records the sending of an expeditionary force.

"*After the full moon, two thousand Spartans arrived at Athens, having made such an effort to reach it that they were in Attica on the third day out of Sparta. They were too late for the battle, but nonetheless they wished to see the Persians.*

Arriving at Marathon, they saw them. Then they departed again, praising the Athenians and their achievement."

Herodotus, Histories 6.120

The speed with which the Spartans reached Athens should remove all doubt of their sincerity. Equally, their inclusion in the Oath of Marathon shows that they were committed to supporting the Athenians against the Persian threat. So something clearly prevented the Spartans from fulfilling their oath and mobilising immediately.

The thriving pottery industry of Athens, such a wonderful pictorial source, was much less well-developed in Sparta. This drinking bowl shows a column of Spartans carrying their dead home. Constant warfare was a perilous drain on the small population of full Spartiates, hence the importance of carefully selecting when to go to war. Mid 6th century BC, now in the Altes Museum, Berlin.

In the official version, Cleomenes had turned traitor, first removing his co-regent Demaratus by underhand means, and then ingratiating himself with the Arcadians for the purpose of making trouble in Sparta. Thankfully, Cleomenes' madness and death had solved that particular problem. Meanwhile, in Athens, the Aeginetan hostages could only be freed on the say-so of two Spartan kings, but only Leotychidas was still alive; and in Sparta, the townsfolk could settle down to celebrate the Carneia festival. Unfortunately, it coincided with the Persian landing at Marathon, so the Spartan army could not be mobilised in time.

However, piecing together other facts and theories, we can start to suggest an entirely different scenario; one in which Cleomenes worked tirelessly to prepare Sparta and Athens for the imminent Persian threat. First, he removed Demaratus, an obvious Persian sympathiser who might have persuaded Sparta to medize; then, he strengthened Sparta's position by neutralising Argos and binding Arcadia with sacred oaths; but he neglected to deal with Messene. In the meantime, he worked to strengthen Athens as well, by seizing hostages from Aegina, a dangerous Persian sympathiser at Athens' back door, and by seeking support in Thessaly; although none materialised, the Athenians may have been encouraged to look for assistance from "other allied towns" there, when they drew up their oath, binding them to Sparta and Plataea.

Why, then, were the Spartans late for Marathon? And why doesn't Herodotus name the commander of their expeditionary force? Spartan society was notoriously secretive, especially concerning events that might be regarded as shameful. It is entirely possible that, in 490 BC, Sparta was in crisis; if not from the Third Messenian War, which we have seen may well have broken out at precisely this time, then from events surrounding Cleomenes' movements, which seem to have been misunderstood by Herodotus and quite possibly by the Spartans themselves.

The story of Cleomenes' end is a bizarre one, in which, confined in his madness to a wooden pillory, he managed to slash himself to death. (Herodotus describes the event at 6.75.2-3.) Many scholars have doubted its veracity, but its timing is equally problematic. Did it occur before the Battle of Marathon, as Herodotus implies, or afterwards? Could Cleomenes have been the commander of the expeditionary force, or was it his Agiad successor, Leonidas? (Of course, there are other possibilities, for the movements of the Eurypontid Leotychidas remain equally unknown.)

If we assume that, days before the Persian landing at Marathon, this was the very moment when the Spartans assassinated their king for his imagined treachery, or perhaps the very moment when their king fell in battle against the Messenians (hardly a worthy enemy), all the more reason for Herodotus' sources to keep quiet.

These conclusions must remain speculative, but one thing is certain: the lack of evidence, combined with the proverbial Spartan secrecy, ensures that we shall never know exactly why the Spartans were late for the Battle of Marathon. ●

Duncan B. Campbell is a regular contributor to Ancient Warfare.

Further Reading
- A. Andrewes, 'Athens and Aegina, 510-480 B.C.', in: *Annual of the British School at Athens* 37 (1936/37), pp. 1-7.
- G.L. Cawkwell, 'Cleomenes', in: *Mnemosyne* 46.4 (1993), pp. 506-527.
- T.J. Figueira, 'The Chronology of the Conflict between Athens and Aegina in Herodotus Bk. 6', in: *Quaderni Urbinati di Cultura Classica* 28.1 (1988), pp. 49-89.
- P.M. Krentz, 'The Oath of Marathon, not Plataia?', in: *Hesperia* 76 (2007), pp. 731-742.

Despite its magnificent reputation, Sparta was hardly invincible, as this sauroter, a spear-butt, attests. Found at the sanctuary of Zeus in Olympia, it commemorates a victory of the island people of Methana over the Lacedaemonians. Copy, now in the Römisch-Germanisches Zentralmuseum, Mainz, Germany.

The aftermath of Marathon

The rise and fall of Athens and Persia

"[The Athenians were]....the first who dared to look without flinching at Persian dress and the men who wore it" (Herodotus 6.115). As the weary Athenian hoplites rested in the precinct of Herakles at Athens in September 490 BC, watching the Persian fleet sail way over the horizon, they were doubtless euphoric at their victory, and the knowledge that they had saved their city.

By Paul McDonnell-Staf

In truth however, it is unlikely the Persians intended to destroy Athens. The force sent was too weak to besiege the city, and it is far more likely that their strategy was to burn and ravage the countryside at harvest time, blockade the city with their fleet and thus starve it into surrendering and accepting the tyrant Hippias once more, becoming a subject city of Persia. Darius would thereby obtain a foothold in the West comparatively cheaply.

Shortly afterward, they were doubtless feasted and feted as the saviours of Athens, and could swell with pride in the knowledge that they were all heroes, lauded as the equals of all those mythology, for had they not performed a miracle by beating in battle the hitherto invincible Persians? They had successfully defied the King of Kings, to whom resistance was futile.

Like all major events, the battle of Marathon had far-reaching consequences for the future, spreading like ripples across a pond...

Consequences for Athens

The first consequence became apparent within days when the promised Spartan help, in the form of 2,000 hoplites, finally arrived having covered 150 miles in

Xerxes, or rather 'the prince', the counterpart to the image of Darius shown before. Originally at the north stairs of the apadana of Persepolis, now in the National Archaeological Museum, Tehran, Iran.

© Livius.org

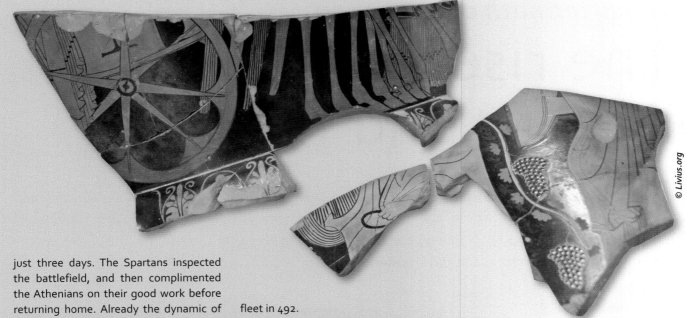

© Livius.org

just three days. The Spartans inspected the battlefield, and then complimented the Athenians on their good work before returning home. Already the dynamic of power in southern Greece was changing for the Athenians now began to see themselves as the equals of the much-vaunted Spartans. Even Sparta had not faced down the invincible Great King and his vast empire on the battlefield. Very shortly, the 'Hero of the Hour', Miltiades, asked for and received 70 triremes together with troops and money to launch an expedition against the island of Paros. The thrifty Athenians saw in this piratical raid a chance to recoup their expenses fending off the Persians. Miltiades demanded 100 talents to raise a siege, but ended up failing and returning home empty-handed with a leg injury. The furious Athenians turned on their hero, prosecuting him for 'defrauding the public'. Gangrene set in to his leg injury however, and he died. His son Cimon paid his fine of 50 talents.

Nor did the euphoria last long once it was realised that Darius had not given up his vengeance, and was preparing a large expedition to invade Greece, instead of a mere punitive raid against Athens and Eretria as a first step in incorporating the *Yauna Paradraya* ("Ionians-over-the-sea", mainland greeks) into his Empire. Fortunately for Greece, and Athens in particular, there was a respite. Encouraged by Athens' successful resistance the already restive Egyptians broke into revolt, followed by other parts of the Empire, and in the meantime Darius died. Thus it was his son Xerxes who amassed the huge army which finally crossed into Greece in 480 BC, having built two bridges of boats across the Dardanelles and dug a canal across the Athos peninsula to remove the threat that had destroyed Mardonius'

fleet in 492.

These were massive engineering feats that took years to plan and complete. In the meantime, the reprieve bought by Marathon had produced a lucky strike of silver at Laureion in Attica. Urged on by Themistocles and others, Athens had built a fleet which by 480 BC numbered some 200 triremes. Marathon had made the Athenians realise how vulnerable they were to attack from the sea, and the utilisation of their new-found wealth to build the fleet and its necessary infrastructure set them irreversibly on the path of maritime empire, ironically not in the interests of the 'Heroes of Marathon', the hoplite farmers of Attica.

When Xerxes finally launched his massive invasion of Greece it was obvious the allied Greek military resources were no match for Persia's. Athens was evacuated. In anger that the stubborn Athenians, bolstered by memories of Marathon already turning to legend, refused to yield, Xerxes burnt the city down including the sacred temples on the Parthenon. He had completed his father's revenge.

However, the season was rapidly running out and a further setback in the form of a naval defeat at Salamis did not help. The stubborn resistance and inevitable delays meant that Persia's logistics, stretched to the limit, broke down. The fleet needed to return before the Autumn gales arrived, and Xerxes needed to return to Asia to forestall the inevitable problems that had arisen in his absence. Mardonius was left with an 'adequate' force to hold down the newly acquired satrapy, and finish off the Peloponnesians and city-less Athenian exiles. The following year

Fragments of painted pottery from the Athenian Acropolis. The discoloration was caused by fire, in this case the fire started by the Persians when they burnt the temple complex down on capturing the city in 480 BC. Now in the National Archaeological Museum, Athens.

the united allies defeated and killed Mardonius at Plataea. A further Persian defeat occurred at Mycale, opposite the island of Samos (479 BC). This was actually the only 'decisive' battle of the Persian Wars, for the Persian fleet was taken and burnt (apart from the Phoenicians and Egyptians, who had returned home), handing naval supremacy of the Aegean to the Greeks.

Athens, thanks to the memory of Marathon and the lucky silver strike at Laureion, was now the premier naval power and lost little time in establishing a league of Aegean cities and islands to advance their cause against Persia. The island of Delos, where its treasury was initially kept, ended up giving the league its name.

Over the next 30 years the Athenian-dominated Delian League gradually transformed into an Athenian empire. It would help oust the Persians from Macedon, Thrace, the Aegean islands and the Ionian coast. In 465, Xerxes was murdered, and as his son Artaxerxes took the throne, Egypt predictably revolted again. Athens assisted the Egyptians in 459, but by 454 her forces in Egypt were destroyed. In 460 the first Peloponnesian War broke out, largely fought against Sparta's allies, and at first Athens was successful, notably against Corinth. With the Egyptian disaster Athens had to regroup and the war settled into stalemate. Another disaster occurred in Cyprus, and with the death of Cimon, the Athenians withdrew.

Peace with Persia finally came in 449 BC with the 'Peace of Callias', ending the half-century of warfare, though ancient historians are divided as to whether an actual treaty was signed. Athens could hardly publicly announce such an accord, since it would cease to justify the 'contributions' of the Delian League. Athens, led by Pericles used its newly-found wealth as an empire to rebuild, notably the Acropolis and its premier temple, the Parthenon. By 445, Pericles signed a 'thirty years truce' with the Peloponnesians.

Athens, despite setbacks, was enjoying a Golden Age, but not without tensions. Marathon and the growing legend of how the 'better' social classes had saved Athens, found itself in social conflict with the 'lower' social classes, the *thetes*, the lowest property class, who were conscious that it was they, as the sailors of Athens fleet, who really generated and maintained Athens' Aegean empire.

In 431, a second and more famous Peloponnesian War broke out. Sparta invaded Attica, and the countryside was abandoned with everyone crowding into the city. A terrible plague broke out as a result and among the many casualties was Pericles himself. Athens, protected by its 'Long Walls' between the city and its harbours, was immune to Peloponnesian land power, while her naval might allowed her to strike back with impunity. However, only a major defeat on land could bring Athens victory. By 422 this war too petered out into a truce. In 418, Athens broke the truce to aid Argos against Sparta, but failed to fully support its allies at the battle of Mantinea which Sparta won. The Athenians thus

Bust of Pericles (c.495-429 BC). Though the Athenian democracy meant, in theory, no one man could control the city's policies, Pericles was one of the most dominant politicians and generals during the Athenian Golden Age. Now in the Altes Museum, Berlin, Germany.

lost their best chance of a land victory over Sparta, but they had their eyes on more profitable aims, and in 416 resolved to invade Sicily, the richest place in the Mediterranean. This campaign would also end in disaster for Athens. In 413 the expedition with all it encompassed, its fleet, and its leaders, was destroyed.

During all this time both sides sought the help of Persia against their fellow Greeks, making a mockery of the idealism of Marathon and the Persian War, and the subsequent 'crusade' against Persia to liberate the Ionian Greeks.

By 405 BC, Sparta, with the aid of Persian gold, finally defeated Athens at sea at Aegospotami in the Dardanelles and Athens' days of greatness were numbered. Sparta, under its King Agesilaus

now had hegemony of Greece in Athens' place, and campaigned in Asia Minor against Persia.

Athens in turn now became Persia's ally. Greek aspirations, the heroic legacy of Marathon, and the Athenian empire all finally came to an end with the shameful 'King's Peace', dictated by the Great King in 387 BC, by which all of Ionia and Cyprus were abandoned to Persian rule, and independent autonomy imposed on the Greek city-states. If Persia had not actually conquered Greece, the Great King could at least briefly claim all Greece was within his sphere of influence.

Consequences for Persia

Persia, like all empires, needed to expand in order to prosper. Having burst westward from Mesopotamia, and absorbed Egypt, the Levant including Phoenicia, and Greek Ionia, Darius was bent on expanding further west into Europe. For geographical reasons, expansion east into India was impractical due to the mountains and deserts of Afghanistan. Expansion north into the 'empty' steppes was also impractical, and no expansion south was possible due to seas and deserts. The west, with its civilisation and rich cities, was an irresistible target for the invincible Great King. While contemplating this, in 499 BC, the *Yauna tyaiye ushkahya* ("Ionians of the land") revolted at the instigation of Aristagoras, governor of Miletus. He sought help from his Greek cousins across the sea with the aid of a bronze map of the world. The Spartans decided Persia was too far away, but Athens and Eretria sent help. In 498, the allies marched, and besieged Sardis, the greatest city in the empire, formerly capital of the Lydian Empire under Croesus, and terminus of the Persian Royal road. Whether by accident or design, the city was fired by the *Yauna*. The fire forced the inhabitants and Persians into the central market square, but the fire was unstoppable and there were thousands of casualties in all probability, as well as the loss of the temples, including the great temple of Cybele, the moon goddess.

Darius was outraged by this sacrilege in addition to the burning of his prized city. By 494 the Ionians had been subdued and punished, and by 492 the Persians under Mardonius had crossed

© Karwansaray Publishers

Tombstone of Sosias Kephisodoros, dating to the late 5th century BC. It illustrates nicely the increase in lightened equipment of the hoplite, now lacking body armor and greaves The traditional equipment also continued to be worn. Now in the Pergamon Museum, Berlin, Germany.

the Hellespont, and had taken Thrace and Macedonia (the *Yauna Takabara*, "Ionians who wear shield shaped sunhats") and the satrapy of Skudra was established. Darius was poised to occupy Greece, and had a perfect *casus belli* in punishing the Athenians and Eretrians for the part they had played in the sacrilegious destruction of Sardis. At this point things went wrong and Mardonius' fleet was lost in a storm off Cape Athos. Around this time the deposed tyrant of Athens, Hippias, appeared at the Persian court and told Darius that if restored in Athens, he would become a loyal subject. Darius seized the opportunity and sent a modest (by Persian standards) expedition, which was almost completely successful in bringing the Aegean islands into the Empire, taking and burning Eretria and deporting the population, and then they made that fateful landing at Marathon, where they received a minor setback...

Artaphernes and the family of the heroically deceased Datis were suitably rewarded for their success, but for Darius there was still some unfinished business with Athens, which could not, for all sorts of reasons, be allowed to successfully defy the Great King's omnipotent will. A larger force would be necessary, and that meant heavier taxes, not to mention the fact that Darius had embarked on expanding his new capital city, Persepolis. That in turn sparked an already rumbling revolt in Egypt, and Darius died to be succeeded by his son Xerxes, who crushed the Egyptian revolt (and others) and continued building Persepolis. Persia was a nation with a military culture that had existed on conquest for several generations, and its empire was geared economically to supplying and supporting this military machine, rather like the twentieth century 'military/industrial complexes' of Germany, Russia or the United States, all of which thrived in an era of warfare. Xerxes had little choice but to continue his father's preparations to punish Athens and expand westward on an even bigger scale, with the results set out above.

After the repulse of Xerxes massive invasion in 479 BC, for Persia the *Yauna Paradraya* ("Ionians across the sea") across the Aegean became a frontier problem, whose dangerous military and naval skills needed to be contained. Persia, a land power, never fully appreciated sea power, although some of its subjects, such as the Phoenicians, certainly did. The Persian aim was now to secure sovereignty over the Ionians in Anatolia. In the meantime Athenian naval power allowed it to nibble away at coastal Persian possessions all around Anatolia, both in the Aegean and the Black sea, and create its empire. The Athenian threat was so great that Persian *satraps* took care to establish themselves well inland, and not near the dangerous coast.

In 465 Xerxes was murdered and succeeded by his son Artaxerxes. The Persians had already learned in their dealings with Ionian city-states that all were rivals, and that within a city-state there were invariably factions who supported the wealthy and oligarchies or tyrants, and the less wealthy majority, who were generally democrats. Persia had exploited these factors and employed a policy of divide and rule. Rather than once again build an expensive navy and confront Athens with no certainty as to the outcome, they now applied these principles and strategies to the Greek mainland states – a more economic, and certainly surer way to curb

these dangerous enemies. As early as 459 BC, Artaxerxes sent an ambassador with much gold to try and lobby Sparta into invading Attica as a counter to Athenian assistance to rebellious Egypt during the first Peloponnesian War.

After the 'Peace of Callias' between Artaxerxes I of Persia and Athens was agreed in 449 BC, war broke out again between the upstart Athenian empire and the former leading power Sparta in 431 over Thebes' attempted annexation of Plataea: the second Peloponnesian War. Artaxerxes tried to lobby and bribe again in 425, but his ambassador was intercepted by the Athenians. The envoy carried a message acidly saying that the Spartans didn't seem to know what they wanted – would they please send someone to clarify? It also seems that, to further his own ends, the Great King established permanent embassies and legations in the major Greek *poleis*, and of course the normal trade flowed from the Middle East into and beyond Greece. All this gave plenty of scope for Persia to carefully play off *polis* against *polis*, and within the cities, oligarchic factions against democratic ones. Ironically, Persia supported democrats more often than oligarchs, for in Persian experience it was the latter who, with a lot of power concentrated in few hands, were more likely to rebel or cause trouble. When Artaxerxes died in 424 BC, the Achaemenid empire had lasted well over a century, and there had been no major conflict between Persia and Greeks for over twenty years, despite the extension of Athens maritime empire onto the coasts of Asia Minor.

Marathon and Xerxes' defeat had also tarnished the omnipotent reputation of the Great King, and when Artaxerxes I was assassinated, an unseemly succession battle broke out between his three illegitimate sons, from which Ochus emerged as Darius II. Various *satraps* in the west also plotted and rebelled, and there were the inevitable revolts of subject nations. Persia was no longer as monolithic as it had been in the great days of Darius I and Xerxes.

Athens seized the opportunity to intervene in Persian politics and play the same game in response. In 414 the city supported a rebellion by the Persian Amorges on the Ionian coast against Darius II. Perhaps this intervention was intended to distract Persia at a time when things were critical

for Athens – her Sicilian expedition would end in complete disaster within a year. In hindsight this proved a huge mistake, for Darius II Ochus now committed to intervening in the second Peloponnesian War from 412 BC on with Athens weakened by the Sicilian disaster. His 'archers' (Gold 'Daric' coins had a Persian archer on the reverse) would prove fatal in the downfall of the Athenian empire. At first, both sides lobbied the Persians through the *satraps* Tissaphernes and Pharnabazos, with Alcibiades of Athens promising an overthrow of the aggressive democrats and a return to oligarchy if Persia would aid him. Alcibiades' byzantine machinations and self-interest soon landed him in trouble. Tissaphernes was inclined to help first one side then the other, whichever seemed in Persia's best interest _ to keep the war going. Matters changed with the arrival of the Great King's son Cyrus, who struck up a friendship with the Spartan Lysander. Persian money assisted Sparta to build ships, and by hiring rowers, man a navy comparable in quality to Athens' own, and defeat her at Aegospotami. With the loss of the Hellespont and the vital food route to the Black Sea, Athens was besieged and starved into submission in 404 BC. The Athenian empire was finished, never to recover.

Beyond the Peloponnesian War

The ending of the war freed thousands of Greek mercenaries onto the market – a potential problem for Sparta's new hegemony, but Darius II Ochus died the same year, and it quickly became apparent that Cyrus intended to rebel against his elder brother Artaxerxes II – and looked to Sparta for help, doubtless the quid pro quo for Cyrus' aid against Athens. Consequently the famous Ten Thousand, composed largely of unemployed Greeks, accompanied Cyrus in his bid for the throne in 401. Their adventurous return after the death of Cyrus at the battle of Cunaxa was told by Xenophon.

Greek mercenary hoplites were another legacy of Marathon and the Persian Wars, for 'hoplite' fame naturally spread and they were in demand with Persian *satraps* and rebels against Persia alike. Even Greek *poleis* hired out their troops in this lucrative trade. The highest number recorded was rebel Egypt in 344 BC with perhaps as many as 20,000 Greek hoplites who were opposed by Persia with

© Karwansaray Publishers

Detail of the so-called Nereid Monument. In this, the tomb of Arbinas, ruler of Xanthos in western Lycia, various elements come together. Xanthos was an Ionian city, formerly part of the Delian League, but at the time of this ruler's death, about 370 BC, again part of the Persian empire. Despite that, the idea of the hoplite as a superior soldier is clearly borne out in this monument. Now in the British Museum, London.

14,000. These numbers were as high as any that had fought a battle in Greece, and the 'Persian' hoplites prevailed over the 'Egyptian' ones, ultimately restoring Egypt to Persia.

The fact that grandee *satraps* such as Tissaphernes and Pharnabazus could act semi-independently was an ominous sign that the cracks were running deep in the Achaemenid empire, and Tissaphernes had done neither Persia nor his king any favours by first treacherously attacking the Ten Thousand, earning the hatred of many Greeks, and then failing to destroy them, demonstrating Persia's military weakness in the face of a Greek hoplite army once more.

In 399, Agesilaus became king of Sparta, and led a Spartan army into Asia Minor against Persia. By 395, Corinth, Argos, Thebes and a resurgent Athens all united against Sparta, backed by Persian money, and the Athenian admiral Conon was appointed commander of a *Persian* fleet, which in 394 inflicted a shattering defeat on the Spartan navy at Cnidus, near Rhodes. In 393, Persian money rebuilt Athens' Long Walls. By 387 Sparta's attempt at empire had been foiled, and the Great King imposed the 'King's Peace', also called the 'Peace of Antalcidas' after the Spartan envoy. All of Asia Minor was acknowledged as belonging to the Great King, and he declared all the Greek cities to be independent, underwritten by his guarantee (save those of the helots of Sparta). Persia's policy to divide and rule had seemingly triumphed. With its

frontier problem solved at last, Persia now turned its attention to recovering Cyprus and Egypt, where Athenian generals like Chabrias and Iphicrates still served the Egyptians as mercenaries. Alas for Persia, the various western *satraps* now revolted against the king, and matters became chaotic with rebellions breaking out in many places. In 361 BC, the aging Spartan king Agesilaus, accompanied by 1,000 Spartan mercenaries and the Athenian Chabrias with more mercenaries sought to wrest the Levant from Persia on behalf of Egypt. Agesilaus died the following year aged 84, on his way home with 230 talents in pay for Sparta. His contemporary, Artaxerxes II also died after reigning 46 years, to be succeeded by Artaxerxes III Ochus who, of necessity in the chaos, gained a reputation for bloodthirstiness, in dealing with Persia's internal troubles for the next twenty years. Artaxerxes III once more tried to regain Egypt and eventually succeeded with the aid of his commanders: Bagoas the eunuch and two Rhodian mercenaries, Mentor and his brother Memnon, the latter of whom with his Greek hoplite mercenaries would eventually face Alexander. A new power among the *Yauna* had arisen: Macedon. In 336 BC, the ruthless Artaxerxes III Ochus died, probably a few months after the assassination of Philip of Macedon, in whose death he may have played a part. He was succeeded by his cousin Kodomannos, who took the title Darius III.

He was destined to be the last Achaemenid King.

Other Greek states

As we have seen Sparta, as proud leader of southern Greece, came to Athens' aid at Marathon, but proved to be too late. As a result, Athens gained all the credit for repelling the Great King and excited the envy of Sparta. However, despite the growing prestige of Athens, it was Sparta that was elected to lead the southern Greek alliance in resisting Xerxes' invasion, though that resistance was inspired by the example of Marathon. Once Xerxes' armies were driven out, Sparta returned to her interests in the Peloponnese. In 464 there was a major earthquake disaster at Sparta, promptly followed by a helot revolt. Spartans may have grown uneasy at the rise of Athens maritime empire, but there was little they could do, pre-occupied as they were with their own problems until 460. However, not long after, and following various tensions between Peloponnesians and Athenians, the first Peloponnesian War broke out, quickly exacerbated by Artaxerxes' bribing Sparta to invade Attica. As related above, the wars lasted until Athens' final defeat in 404 BC, with Persia successfully keeping these dangerous Greeks at each others' throats until Cyrus aided final Spartan victory.

This Spartan success immediately exposed the tensions implied in the agreement with Persia, whereby the *hegemon* ("leader") of Greece against Xerxes and now self-proclaimed liberator of the Greeks had abandoned the Greeks of Asia to the Great King in exchange for Persian gold. This problem had always been present, for many Spartans took their role as protector of Greek 'freedom' seriously. Hence Spartan dithering in early negotiations with Persia referred to above, and even after pragmatism had prevailed, there were always those like the admiral Callicratidas who objected to flattering barbarians for the sake of money. Once Sparta got what she wanted and triumphed, this faction prevailed, and Sparta reneged on her agreement by annexing many of the Ionian cities and compounded this breach by assisting (unofficially) the rebellion of Cyrus against his brother Artaxerxes II in 401 BC.

Spartan hegemony did not last long, and Agesilaus' attempt at empire through conquest of Asia Minor failed when the other Greek states, including a re-nascent Athens, ganged up against her, supported by Persia. In Greece, the 'King's Peace' did not last long, when Thebes aided by Athens, went to war with Sparta in 378. As Thebes began to dominate, especially after Epaminondas' victory at Leuktra in 371, Athens switched sides and joined her old foe Sparta.

The consequences of the Battle of Marathon for Macedon and Thrace, already incorporated into a Persian satrapy, and then the states of central Greece following Xerxes invasion, were not too severe. The success of the allies in driving off the Persians, followed by Athens' rise as maritime power led to Persian domination being short-lived. In fact, Macedon prospered from Athens' decision to build a navy for the timber and raw materials came from there, and it is likely the ships themselves were built at Athenian colonies such as Methone and Amphipolis. This newly found prosperity set Macedon, previously torn by tribal warfare from neighbours and internal strife, on the road to growth and security. Macedon was also relatively untroubled by the southern Greeks, largely thanks to Persia's policy of divide and rule, for no one of them grew powerful enough to absorb Macedonia. Her rise became meteoric after Philip came to power in 359 BC, having learnt much as a hostage in Thebes in his youth. Philip utilised Macedon's ample manpower and recently discovered gold deposits (only Macedon and Persia issued gold coins) to subdue his neighbours and then take over Thrace and finally almost all of Greece. The politically

canny Philip obtained as much by diplomacy as conquest, and like many Greeks was conscious of Persia's weakness after years of rebellions by over-mighty *satraps* and subject nations. His sudden assassination in 336 BC, perhaps instigated by Artaxerxes III Ochus, no stranger to using assassination, did not bring relief to Persia for the young Alexander would inherit his father's invasion force, and with it, destroy Achaemenid Persia.

Conclusion

The Battle of Marathon, that miraculous defeat of the Goliath Persia by the David Athens, had far-reaching consequences for all those involved. For Athens, it brought short term reprieve until Xerxes avenged his father's defeat, but the idea, the myth of the few 'freedom loving' Athenians hurling back the innumerable 'slaves' of the Great King grew and thrived. It inspired Sparta to lead the Peloponnesians and city-less Athenians to successfully resist Xerxes, and they too absorbed the 'Marathon Myth' of upholding 'Greek freedom' against 'tyrannical Persia'. It made Athenians aware of their vulnerability to the sea, in turn leading to Athens becoming a maritime power and Empire. It is worth examining this freedom that Athens in particular extolled. As Thucydides makes clear in his histories, particularly the Melian dialogue, Athens' idea of 'freedom' meant the freedom to do unto others before they did unto you, or:

"The strong do what they have to do, and the weak accept what they must"

And what of the 'freedom' of the Ionian cities that began it all? To them, 'freedom' meant paying tribute to Athens, while 'slavery' meant paying tribute to Persia (and sometimes both at once!). After the 'King's Peace', many in Sparta agonised over selling out the Ionian cities for gold, while Athenian propaganda lambasted them for it. Ironically, the Ionian cities actually benefited from the 'betrayal', because in the chaotic times that followed, archaeology shows them to have thrived and grown, in a semi-independent state. Halicarnassus under its Carian King Mausolus was a good example, for under him the city prospered and when he died

in 353 BC it built him the first 'mausoleum' as a tomb, one of the Seven Wonders of the World.

Politically, Marathon and the awareness of vulnerability to the sea and subsequent naval power meant the democrats triumphed over the oligarchic 'Men of Marathon' and established democracy of a sort in Athens, but in the end, democracy could not match the single-minded purpose of a tyranny or oligarchy and Athens failed and fell.

For Persia, Marathon marked the high water line of her expansion. Her defeat, albeit only a minor setback, led to the even bigger failure of Xerxes, despite Herculean efforts, to incorporate the *Yauna Paradraya* into the empire. This in turn led to stagnation, and thereafter Persia was more concerned with holding the empire together, rather than expanding it. This would be the pattern for all empires. These Marathon threads would all come together – the rise of Greek economic power, thanks in part to injections of Persian money, the rise in Greek military power as a result, and its use by Persia, the psychology of the superiority of the 'hoplite' over 'barbarians', the social changes, the growing awareness that the Great King had feet of clay, the divide and rule policy which undermined the city states and thus allowed the rise of Macedon – and would culminate in a Macedonian empire which would, under Alexander, finally destroy Achaemenid Persia, though it was already decaying.

When Darius proudly sent forth his expedition against Athens to Marathon, as he said on his tomb:

"...then shall it become known to you: the spear of a Persian man has gone forth far; then shall it become known to you: a Persian man has delivered battle far indeed [3,000 km in fact!] from Persia."

He little dreamed that the train of events he was setting in motion would culminate in the destruction of the Achaemenids. ●

Paul McDonnell-Staff is a regular contributor to Ancient Warfare.

The mechanics of hoplite battle

Storm of spears and press of shields

Over the last half century, a schism developed over hoplite combat that has devolved into a *bellum sacrum*, with an orthodoxy assailed by an increasingly popular heresy. The orthodox position, championed by Hanson, Luginbill, and Schwartz, portrays hoplites as lumbering masses of men that charged directly into each other and contested the battlefield by attempting to physically push their foes. Van Wees, Krentz, and Goldsworthy, describe hoplites as closer to skirmishers, fighting in an opened order, and often paired with missile troops. Any 'push' was either a figurative description or uncoordinated shield-bashing. I believe they are both in some measure correct, and often equally wrong.

By Paul Bardunias

This debate has forced historians to stray far from their fields of study. Their arguments suffer from an insufficient understanding of the physics and mechanics of large masses or crowds. Group behavior is my field, and, with the context that I can provide for their arguments, I shall make an attempt at syncretism.

Hoplite equipment

Herodotus was the first author to describe the heavy infantry of ancient Greece as hoplites, or men who were considered fully equipped for battle. A hoplite's arms and armor, his panoply, might have included a bronze helmet, greaves, a bronze cuirasse or corslet of leather or textile, and an iron sword. A rich man might add bronze thigh, upper arm, ankle, and even toe guards. The only pieces that seemed to have been required were the large, round shield or *aspis* and a 1.8-2.5 m thrusting spear. Herodotus contrasts hoplites with *psiloi*, literally "naked", armed with missile weapons.

The panoply of the hoplite emerged in the late 8th century, with the advent of the round, domed, shield and thrusting spear with pointed spear-butts or *sauroters*. It has been suggested that these items indicate a break from earlier, skirmishing and missile combat, but *aspis*-bearing hoplites on some early vases, like the Chigi vase (ca. 640), appear to bear a pair of spears with throwing cords attached, a shorter one most likely to be thrown and a second longer spear which could be thrown or used in close combat.

By the 5th century, the classical Greek *dory*, or fighting spear, appears to have been as much as 2.5 m long, but it was effectively longer because a combination of rear weighting and tapering of the shaft moved the center of balance, hence the grip, back to about a third of the way from the bottom. A 2.5 m *dory* had a reach of over 1.5 m, similar to a 3.3 m mid-balanced spear. The great reach of this spear was a handicap in single combat, because it would be useless if a foe managed to move up shield to shield. A man cannot reach back far enough to bring a point that is 1.5 m from his grip to bear with any force against a foe this close. However, in a battle line, the extra reach enabled hoplites to support the men beside them, the reach of their spears overlapping to a greater extent. Moving within the reach of the combined spears of a phalanx would be much more difficult than evading any single spear.

Hoplite's shield

The shield has also been seen as unsuitable for single combat. The hoplite's shield, the *aspis*, *hoplon*, or perhaps most specifically, Argive *aspis*, varied little in size or shape over the whole period of hoplite warfare. It was made in the form of a flattened dome, some 10 cm deep, between 90 cm to just over a meter in diameter, including a robust, offset rim of some 4-5 cm. The rim, and often the whole face of the shield were covered in a single sheet of bronze, 0.5- 1 mm thick. The orthodoxy reconstructs this shield as exceptionally heavy (7-9 kg), but Krentz has suggested a more likely 6.8 kg or less.

These features are not unique to the Greek shield. A convex shape functions to transfer force away from the site of impact, while an offset rim reinforces the face of the shield so that it does not split when struck. Exceptionally convex shields, conical in profile, are common in many cultures because the profile ensures that an incoming strike will encounter a sloped shield-face.

The *aspis* had an uncommon system of grips that some suggest limited the shield's utility in single combat to the point that men were forced to fight in close order. The left arm was slipped through a bronze cuff, or *porpax*, placed either at the shield's center or just to the right of center. The *porpax* either accepted a leather sleeve or was itself tapered to accept the forearm up to just below the elbow, and fit like the cuff of a modern

© Livius.org

Detail of a drinking bowl showing a fully equipped hoplite and the inside of the aspis, *with the* porpax *just off the center of the shield, and a simple rope grip on the outer edge. Now in the Museum of Art and History, Brussels, Belgium.*

artificial limb, holding the limb so snuggly that the shield would not rotate around the forearm. A second grip near the rim of the shield was gripped by the hand, and tension from this grip acted to hold the arm in the *porpax*. In shields from other cultures that have a double-grip system, the grip for forearm and hand usually flank the center of the shield. This allows most of the shield to be brought up in front of its bearer, while the *aspis* allows only half the shield to cover a man's front. The central placement of the *porpax* in the *aspis* is an advantage, because it makes holding the shield up on the bent forearm easier by reducing the proportion of the shield's mass that is to the right of the elbow and must be pivoted up. A double-grip limits

the range through which a shield can be moved to block. The shield cannot be held as far away from the body as one gripped by the hand, which leaves a greater portion of the body vulnerable to incoming strikes and reduces the distance a strike must penetrate to wound. It has been suggested that hoplites could gain coverage by standing perpendicular to shields in a 'fencers' stance. This analogy is untenable because fencers lead with their weapon hand, while hoplites would have to come up parallel to their shields to effectively strike with their spears.

The *aspis* has one unique feature that is difficult to explain. The Bomarzo shield in the Vatican's Museo Gregoriano Etrusco, which retains large portions of its wooden

core, presents an odd picture. The shield's core is only 5-6 mm thick over much of the shield's face, thickening to 8 mm in the center where the *porpax* was affixed. Near the rim of the bowl, the shield curves back sharply to form side-walls of 10-14 mm that taper towards the shield face. Blythe's analysis adds a third to the thickness due to shrinkage, but the width of the side-walls relative to face remains.

A shallow dome tends to spread outward under pressure, and the wide, perpendicular rim acts to keep the face from splitting. But the side-wall section is not thickened in that plane. Under pressure, an *aspis* will fail where the side-wall and the face join. This odd profile has inspired the suggestion that the *aspis*' great weight

Hoplites advancing with brandished spears and raised shields. Note the perpendicular side-wall section between the shallow dome of the face of the shield and the offset rim.

required this curve to allow a man to carry the shield on his shoulder. Leaving aside that the *aspis*' mass has probably been overestimated, some rough calculations show that this explanation is unlikely. The *aspis*' weight did not likely motivate the curved outer portion because, even though only 3-4 cm wide, the greater thickness and large diameter of the 'ring' of wood that makes up the side-wall section accounts for 20-40% of the total mass of wood making up the shield-face! Reinforced side-walls could provide added protection against chopping blows by swords, but this would be superfluous given the thick, bronze covered rim. The side-walls appear to add more depth to the shield than strength, a function we will return to later.

Modern authors present us with irreconcilable images of how these early *aspis*-bearers fought. To some there was a 'hoplite revolution' and orderly phalanxes either closely follow or predate the new shield. Van Wees describes a 'motley crew' of intermingled hoplites, archers, and horsemen that slowly transitions from bands of warriors to the phalanx familiar to 5th century historians. Tyrtaeus, a 7th century Spartan poet, wrote to inspire the warriors of his polis. Two themes run through his works: he chides his audience to stand close to their fellows and to bring the fight to close quarters with their foes. Tyrtaeus can easily be interpreted as a

herald for the classical hoplite phalanx, with close ordered ranks and files. But if men were formed in an orderly phalanx, why would the poet need to deride skulkers who remained out of the range of missiles?

Order versus chaos

This dichotomy of order-vs-chaos is a hot topic in the physical sciences, and the boundary between the two has diminished. Order within groups can arise spontaneously from seemingly random acts of individuals. We call this process self-organization. Through this mechanism, swarms, flocks, herds and schools of animals achieve levels of coordinated movement that any human drillmaster would envy. Swarms, or crowds, of humans are capable of this type of organization as well. If we take Van Wees' 'motley crew' and add simple, logical rules like "archers tend to stand behind men with shields" and "men with shields tend to stand beside men with shields to protect their flanks", then we end up with a formation that resembles the Germanic shield-wall or late Roman *foulkon*. This type of formation puts more heavily armored men, who may throw missiles themselves, in front of unarmored missile troops to act as a wall or screen. Segregation like this is natural in tribal war bands, where richer, better-equipped men lead a troupe of progressively poorer equipped warriors into

battle. It would actually take more discipline to keep troop types evenly mixed than to clump in this manner.

There is no need for hoplites to form in a particularly opened order to allow men to move freely through such a self-organized group. One advantage of the large diameter of the *aspis* is that it acted as a literal meter-stick. Men did not need to make any judgment on their frontage beyond lining up shield rim to shield rim. In human crowds, as in schools of fish or flocks of birds, individuals are completely interchangeable. The result is that no one has a specific place in the formation and the group is highly fluid. Men can move to the front line or beyond to throw missiles at the enemy or challenge a foe, then melt back into the group and retire out of combat. Such 'milling' is commonly seen in all but the densest of crowds.

When two crowds come into contact, the dynamic changes and the presence of one lends order to the other. The limitation on forward movement and the presence of the enemy line as a focal point for the men in both mobs results in the crowd becoming denser as men pile up. If the men at the front-line between the groups are shield to shield, then the literal pushing of mass on mass envisioned by the orthodoxy could ensue. Thus, a crowd like this can be both flexible enough to allow all of the missile combat and personal challenges seen in the pre-hoplite era and spontaneously form into compressed masses akin to phalanxes upon contact with the enemy. Men who are free to move forward and back are also free to flee at the first setback. This can be mitigated by forming men up next to their relatives or in smaller units, where leaving would be noticed. To form the ordered ranks and files that made up the classical phalanx, each man needed to know only who he stood next to or behind

If the economies of the Greek cities allowed for increasing numbers of warriors and a higher percentage of these were well armed hoplites, then a shift from a few ranks of men acting to shield lighter troops to deep ranks of spearmen who charge swiftly to spear range may simply emerge from the conditions of the battlefield rather than result from an intentional tactical shift. As the number of men increased, additional depth would be easier to coordinate than a widely extended battle line. If the percentage of missile troops dropped low, or the defenses of the hoplites reached a level of protection that charging through an enemies' missile barrage was less risky than engaging in a missile duel, then the move to an all hoplite phalanx would result. Once hoplites began to form in more than four ranks, missile troops became ineffective. Xenophon (Anabasis 3.3.7) describes the difficulty of bowmen in firing over the ranks of their own hoplites.

Increasing the depth of phalanxes is advantageous in close combat for a variety of physical and psychological reasons. The heretical view holds that the ranks beyond the first one or two do not directly participate in battle, but play an important role in supporting the front ranks in battle. Beyond acting as a reserve, ready to step forward over the fallen rankers in front of them, the mere presence of these men behind the front rankers raises the morale of those men fighting. In addition, deep ranks of men formed behind the fighting front limit the ability of those men to turn and run.

In the orthodox view, all of the ranks run together into battle as a single mass, then crash into the formation of their foes. This physical pushing match, for which the term *othismos* has been applied, has been likened to a giant rugby scrum, with the goal of pushing the opposing section of the phalanx out of alignment with the rest of the formation until they rout. I believe that a pushing match did occur in hoplite battle, but I am sympathetic to the heretics because the physics of *othismos* have been misstated by the orthodoxy.

The press

Othismos is a noun that derives from the word *otheo*, a verb meaning "to thrust, push, or shove". The modern definitions of *othismos* treat the noun *othismos* as a verb, for example Liddell and Scott render it as either "thrusting, pushing" or secondarily "jostling, struggling". As a noun, the word would have to be defined as "a state wherein thrusting, pushing, jostling or struggling occurs". We commonly call such a state a dense crowd. Perhaps the best English equivalent would be the way we derive a state of dense crowding, a press, from the verb "to press." This is not a crowd in the sense of many people or a throng, because the Greeks had other words to describe that. It is essentially a traffic term, like jam or deadlock, implying that many individuals are locked together and cannot move past. Crowds can 'push' with extreme force, but the word focuses on density, more of a squeeze directed within the group than without.

Othismos is used primarily in three ways. First, it is used to describe hoplite battle. Thucydides (4.96.2) describes fierce combat, noting that it is accompanied by *othismos aspedon*. This description has been held up as the clearest evidence for *othismos* as "pushing with shields", but perhaps a better reading is a *deadlock of shields*, emphasizing the crowding of the opposing ranks together, with or without pushing. Arrian (*Tactica* 12.3) much later used the same word to describe not opposing ranks, but the crowding of second rankers in a phalanx against the backs of the front rankers, after which they can reach the enemy front rankers with their swords.

Second, *othismos* is used in situations familiar to anyone studying crowd disasters. In the worst of these, people are asphyxiated or squeezed either hard enough or long enough to cause them to lose consciousness or die because pressure on their chest and diaphragm prevents them from breathing. Xenophon (A. 5.2.17), Plutarch (Brutus 18.1), and Appian (*Mithridatic wars* 10.71) all describe *othismos* occurring as a crowd of men attempt to exit a gate. Polybius (4.58.9) describes the Aegiratans routing the Aetolians who fled into a city: "in the confusion that followed the fugitives trampled each other to death at the gates...Archidamus was killed in the struggle and crush at the gates. Of the main body of Aetolians, some were trampled to death..." It is known that most deaths attributed to trampling are in fact due to asphyxia while still standing.

The third use of *othismos* occurs where literal pushing could not occur. When Plutarch (Aristides 9.2) describes ships in *othismos*, he refers to crowding, not mass pushing. In many cases, *othismos* is completely figurative. Herodotus twice (8.78, 9.26) uses *othismos* to describe an argument. This is often translated as a "fierce argument", but traffic terms are commonly used to describe arguments. For example, we regularly call for an arbiter when two sides in negotiation come to an impasse. At Plataea, the Tegeans and Athenians (Herodotus 9.26) found themselves at an impasse in negotiations because they both put forth equal claims

A hoplite armed only with shield, spear and helm. Shield faces were decorated with blazons that identified individuals or their polis, while serving to draw the eyes of their foes in combat. Detail of a large crater depicting either Herakles and Argonauts or perhaps the battle of Marathon. Painted the by the Niobid painter, mid 5th century BC, now in the Louvre, Paris.

to an honored place in the army's formation.

The definition of *othismos* does not of itself require a coordinated push of all ranks against an enemy formation, but I believe there was such a concerted struggle of mass against mass. The orthodoxy portrays hoplites as charging as much as 50 m in order to impart what Schwartz termed "a maximum of penetration power at the collision." However, the whole notion that hoplites charged like un-horsed medieval knights to maximize

© Karwansaray Publishers

A Salpinx player leading warriors on the march or exhorting them to battle shown on an Athenian Lekythos, a type of container often found in funerary contexts and usually displaying funerary related themes from about 480 BC, now in the Walters Museum of Art, Baltimore, MD.

the mass' force during a collision is a fallacy. It takes only a few yards to achieve 'ramming speed', and any excess distance causes fatigue and loss of cohesion. They would be correct if the goal was to maximize the force of one man colliding with another, but the physics of maximizing the aggregate force of a group of individuals is different. Dense packing is far more important to transfer a strong, sustainable force, even if it occurs at slow speed. If a hoplite phalanx charged directly into a pushing match, it would have closed up all of the men in the files, belly to back in the manner I have previously described (Bardunias 2007) and charge from very short range to minimize the loss of cohesion.

Reverse tug-o-war

The common description of *othismos* as a tug-o-war in reverse leads to some false impressions. The image conjures up men standing perpendicular to their foes, digging in the edge of their rear foot as they lean into the man in front with their shoulders in the bowls of their shields. But in a tug-o-war, the force is transferred through the rope and men can take any stance as long as they pull on the rope. This is not the case with files of men pushing. As men in files pushed against those in front, the force first acted to compress the men in front, and only after they resisted compression could force be transmitted ahead. At moderate levels of compression this was not a problem, but as greater force was transferred forward, the men

could no longer hold their shields away from their bodies and shields became pressed to the torsos.

If men were standing in a side-on stance as portrayed by the orthodoxy, the force would be transferred directly through the shoulders of each man in file. This was unstable because the only thing holding men perpendicular to their shields was the strength of their left arm. Unless the men closed up laterally belly to back, which is impossible with a meter wide *aspis*, the sustained, grinding pressure on their right shoulders would force them to collapse forward until they were parallel to their shields and the men in files were packed belly to back. Once they achieve this spacing and stance, they can be compressed no further and have achieved what specialists on crowd disasters term a 'critical density'. This is defined as at least eight people pressed together with less than 1.5 m of spacing per person. By simply leaning against the man in front like a line of dominoes, 30-75 % of body mass can be conveyed forward in files, and just three leaning men can produce a force of over 792 N or 80 kg. Shock waves can travel through such crowds, and less than ten people have been shown to generate over 4500 N or 450 kg of force.

This has been misunderstood by authors in the past. To counter the objection that the force transferred forward by men in files would be lethal to one's own file-mates, Franz, as quoted by Schwartz, mistakenly put forth that force is not derived from the weight of the men in file, but from their muscular strength in pushing. This is not true. He further quotes Franz as describing why the files did not produce lethal pressure: "When people behind sense that pushing does not produce an immediate advantage, they stop pushing. This results in a kind of reverse thrust." This is surely true for most historical armies, where weapon play, not pushing is the goal, but the whole point of *othismos* as defined by the orthodoxy is to push against the opposite formation with the greatest force. A file of hoplites, even eight deep, could produce enough force to kill a man through asphyxia. A force of 6227 N will kill if applied for only 15 seconds, while 4-6 minutes of exposure to 1112 N is sufficient to cause asphyxia. Hoplites would be purposefully attempting to create and maintain levels of pressure that occur accidentally in crowds. Killing crowds form when people try to move in a specific direction, such as towards a stage or out a door. Hoplites pushed ahead in file, and if whatever was in front of them did not give way, pressure would rapidly build to lethal levels, and by simply leaning forward they could maintain much of this force for extended periods. There is no requirement for containment such as walls alongside the crowds as we usually see in disasters. As long as they are pushing towards a common goal, in this case directly toward the enemy through the back of the man in front, they will not disperse laterally.

Shield side-walls

The heretics would be correct in assuming that pushing by deep files was not survivable, but for one detail. In my description of the hoplite shield, I put off discussing the single feature of its construction that appears to be unique - the oddly thickened side-walls. As I noted, it appears to primarily add depth, not strength, when compared to other convex shields. It is this depth that allows a man to survive the press of *othismos*, by protecting his torso from compression. To do so, it would be held directly in front of the body with the right half of the shield resting on the hoplite's upper chest and the front of his left shoulder, the bottom on his left thigh. Most of the men in files would have been standing upright and leaning forward. Only the rear few ranks had enough freedom of movement to assume positions that are compatible with active pushing. Shock waves of the combined weight of the file would be added to the pushing force in the rear rankers in the same manner that the mass of a battering ram is pushed towards a barrier.

Othismos may have originated because men pushed their foes away from fallen leaders to retrieve their corpses and armor. Such struggles are common in the Iliad, and Herodotus used the word *othismos* to describe the struggle over Leonidas's body at Thermopylae (7.225). In what can be seen as an egalitarian shift, victory in hoplite battles generally went to the force that held the battlefield and the bodies of all the fallen men upon it. This could represent a ritualization of warfare, and a means of deciding conflict that minimized slaughter, but it may have been the most efficient means of combat given a preexisting warrior ethos that called for large decisive battles and the retrieval of casualties. Pushing would have evolved gradually from close-in fighting that predated the *aspis*. Mass pushing is not unseen in other settings. For example, the Romans pushed with bosses of their shields at Zama (Livy), but the shape of the *scutum* limited the maximum force that could be generated without killing their own men. A sub-lethal, jostling, shoving crowd must have existed before the *aspis* became specialized for killing crowds. Also, the threat of battle moving to a lethal crowd phase would justify the shape of the shield, even if *othismos* was not the goal of combat. The shield as 'life preserver' in a killing crowd explains the constancy of the shape over time. The deep, flattened dome could not vary much and still retain its ability to resist compression. When the shield was found inadequate protection from missiles, an apron of leather was hung from the round shield rather than remaking the shield into a weaker oval that would provide the same coverage.

Hoplite battle

The remainder of this article describes the course of hoplite battle in Herotodus's day, reconciling orthodox and heretical views where possible. Athenian hoplites, like those of most *poleis*, called up amateur levies according to tribal units called *taxeis* of about 700-1000 men, which was then subdivided into *lochoi* of 100 or more. The men may have not had set places in ranks, but by this date they probably knew who they stood next to. These *taxeis* were drawn up alongside one another to form what Thucydides called a *parataxeis* (litterally *taxeis* ranged alongside each other) and others call a phalanx. The Spartans provide us with an example of what was possible with a professional army. Their basic tactical unit was the sworn band or *enomotia* of about forty men, wherein each man knew his assigned place. Ancient authors usually recorded the number of ranks, or shields, men formed in. This seems to have often been up to the unit commander, and could commonly vary from four to sixteen, with eight to twelve being the norm for most of the period. Environmental constraints, like a narrow road, could force units to form in deep ranks by stacking smaller units. Thebans in the late 5th and early 4th century notoriously formed in 25 or even 50 ranks for major battles, an obvious advantage for their contingent, but their allies attempted to limit them to sixteen ranks in the Corinthian war because the sacrifice in frontage left the whole phalanx vulnerable to envelopment.

Once the men were in place, in most armies their leaders would walk along the front haranguing them. Spartans relied on encouragement between hoplites and sang to each other in the ranks. In a prelude to the battle to come, the opposing light troops or cavalry could skirmish in the space between the opposing phalanxes. When the light troops had been recalled and the sacrifices had been taken, the commanders had trumpets, *salpinx*, sounded and men began marching towards the enemy. At this distance men would have been marching with their spears on their right shoulder and their shields on their left. For comfortable carry, the balance point of the spear should be just beyond the shoulder, and many images show hoplites holding the spear down near the *sauroter*. Ancient Greek battlefields were famously flat and not overly broad which allowed men to keep some semblance of order. As they advanced the hoplites sang the Paean in unison, aiding morale and coordination. Marching in step would have been beyond most armies, but the Spartans moved to the sound of pipes to help the men keep pace. At this point men would bring the shield up in front and the command would be passed for the first two ranks to lower spears. This has been interpreted as bringing the spears down to an underarm position, but hoplite reenactors have discovered a simple maneuver to "lower" a *dory* into the overhand position. They let the spear fall forward off the shoulder while at the same time bringing the rear of the spear out and up. There would be no need to shift the grip later if overhand strikes are desired.

Charge to contact

When the armies were less than 180 m apart, most phalanxes shouted an ululating war cry to Enyalius and charged at the run. They did so for psychological reasons, both to channel their nervous tension into the attack, and frighten the enemy with their rapid advance. Coordinating the charge along the chain of units that made up the phalanx seems to have been difficult, and gaps often formed as some hoplites charged sooner than others. Variation

Charging

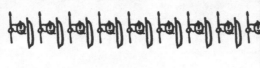

1. All marching. Shields at rest on shoulder and spears upright.

2. Shields brought to front and spears lowered in the two front ranks.

3. Charge begins, men move out, losing a bit of their alignment.

© Andrew Brozyna, ajbdesign.com

Spear Fighting

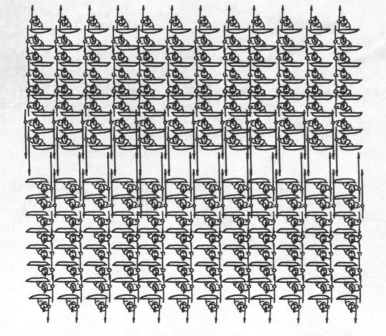

© Andrew Brozyna, ajbdesign.com

in speed of advance could lead to one section of the line leaving the rest running swiftly to catch up (Xenophon, *Anabasis* 1.8.18). Spartans did not charge at the run, but approached in a slow, orderly fashion, so any unit ranged alongside them invariably pulled away when they charged. The result is that a phalanx rarely encountered its opposite as a unified front. For these reasons Thucydides (5.70.1) tells us that large armies are apt to break their order in the moment of engaging.

Thucydides (5.71.1) also describes phalanxes drifting to the right as they advanced because men sought to shelter their unshielded right side. This would have resulted from men twisting their torsos to hold the *aspis* in front of them. It is likely that the whole phalanx contracted as well. Bunching as they moved would have been a natural reaction of frightened men as it is with other animals. The *Strategikon*, attributed to Maurice (12B.17), describes the ease with which men can converge laterally just prior to contact with the enemy. Two approaching phalanxes would end up overlapping on the right through either drift or contraction to the right, and the difference would be difficult to tell. Men who began the charge at a spacing of just over the diameter of their shields might now find that they overlap to some degree with their neighbor's.

Much of the order lost during the charge could be regained as units reformed a battle line upon contact with the enemy. The alternative is that whole *taxeis* ran tens of meters past units next to them in line that were engaged when the foes opposite were delayed or slow moving Spartans. The two phalanxes would have slowed as the enemy loomed large. The same fear that drove them to charge would keep them from running blindly into a hedge of enemy spears. Because disorganized men charging at speed into the enemy results in a weaker mass collision, there is no reason why men could not halt at spear range rather than after crashing together. If men did not regularly stop and fight with their spears, then it is difficult to understand the many references to one phalanx breaking when the two had closed to spear range. Hoplites converging at even a modest 5 mph would cover this distance in less than half a second.

"Storm of spears"

What followed was described by Sophocles (*Antigone*, 670) as a "storm of spears". While taunting their foes, the first two ranks of the opposing phalanxes would assume the ¾ stance common to most combat arts and strike overhand across a gap of about the 1.5 m reach of a dory. The overhand motion results in a much stronger thrust than stabbing underhand (Connolly, 2001), and would be less likely to impale the men behind. When striking from behind a wall of shields, the overhand strike not only ensured that your arm was always above the line of shields but allowed a wide range of targets. During this combat adjacent hoplites were mutually supporting, and a man could be killed through the failure of those adjacent to him (Euripides, *Heracles* 190). The second rankers would have attacked where they could reach, but their spears also acted to defend the men in front.

The *aspis* would have been tilted up and toward the enemy. With the shield snug on the forearm, this would be the natural result of lifting the arm, but it also presents the maximum shield area to a downward, overhand strike. In this position, the shoulder doesn't bear any of the weight because the centrally placed *porpax* results in the lower half of the shield balancing the upper half with all the weight on the arm. It can be braced against the shoulder if pushed back by a strike.

Spear fighting could go on for some time, and often one side must have given way as a result, but we know that battles could move to close range. It is difficult to imagine men easily forcing their way through multiple ranks of massed spears, but we know that hoplites often broke their spears, and a sword armed man would be highly motivated to close within the reach of his foe's spear. Perhaps this was easier as fatigue set in. Once swordsmen closed with the spearmen somewhere along the line, phalanxes could collapse into each other like a zipper closing as spearmen abandoned their useless spears in favor of their own swords.

It is now that rear rankers could bring their pressure to bear. They would close up swiftly, initially supporting those in front, but then gradually pushing them tight together. All ranks would now cover their chests with their shields. While this was occurring the front rankers fought,

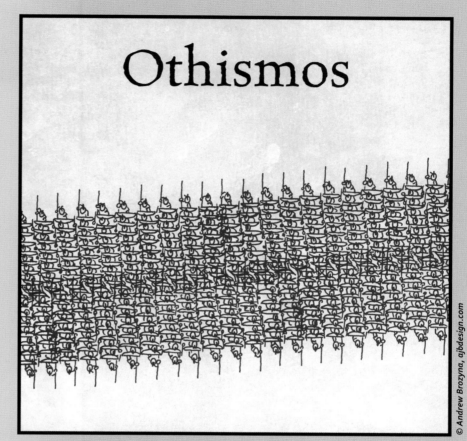

Othismos

© Andrew Brozyna, ajbdesign.com

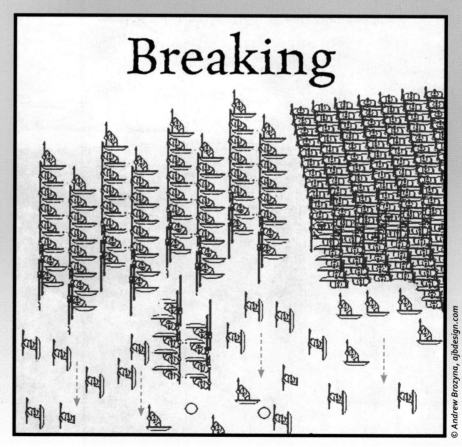

Breaking

© Andrew Brozyna, ajbdesign.com

Iron short sword or dagger with ivory chape. Provenance uncertain, but possibly from Marathon. Now in the British Museum, London.

and their blows could not miss (Xenophon, *Anabasis* 2.1.16). Images of hoplites show a variety of strikes that could be used with the upraised right arm over the shields. The so-called 'Harmodios blow' is a high slash from around the head that has been derided as useless, but here strikes and parries up around the head would be the rule. Point heavy chopping swords would be useful in *othismos*, but the short swords, often attributed to Sparta and seen on stelai from Athens and Boeotia, would be deadly. A downward stab, alongside the neck, into the chest cavity can be seen on a vase in the Museo Nazionale de Spina (T1039A).

Breaking off

The crowding of *othismos* and periods of active, intense pushing could last for a long time as men leaned ahead like weary wrestlers. But the peak pressure is only maintained if the opposing phalanx chooses to resist it. If they move back, their foes have to pack-in tight again before maximum force can be transferred. All such moves have to start at the back of the files, there is no point at which a man could simply jump back and his enemy would fall forward. Just as packing was gradual, so is unpacking. The whole mass would move in spasms and waves like an earthworm. Increased file depth is an advantage in this type of contest, but the answer to those who wonder how, at Leuktra, fifty ranks of Thebans didn't immediately drive twelve ranks of Spartans from the field rests in the difficulty in coordinating such deep files of men to push in unison and the need to constantly repack as men advance. Deep ranks function more like a wall behind those in front than an aid in pushing forwards.

When hoplites could no longer sustain the rigors of pushing, the rear ranks of the phalanx would turn and flee. What followed could be a free for all as men broke ranks to target the backs of routed foes. It was then that the lessons of *hoplomachoi*, martial arts masters, were of most use (Plato, *Laches* 182a). Men who had been holding up their arms throughout battle would surely opt for underhand strikes at this point as seen for single combat on many vases. Hoplites did not press pursuit for long, so many saved their lives by dropping their shields and spears and outpacing those chasing them. Safer still was making a stand with compatriots and letting the victorious hoplites find easier prey as Socrates did after Delium (Plato, *Symposium* 221b).

Hoplite battle encompassed both the storm of spears and press of shields, but by the late 5th century clever generals were coming up with ways of exploiting the weaknesses of both phases of combat. Envelopments and ultra-deep formations took advantage of the weaknesses of armies set on simply fighting a decisive battle with units arrayed opposite them with little regard for flank protection. A century later hoplites would lose their supremacy to Macedonian pikemen, themselves up-armored skirmishers, which presented them with spears that far outranged the *dory* and only a dense hedge of spear points to push against. ●

Paul Bardunias is an entomologist working on self-organized group behavior in termites and ants. His interest in ancient warfare is hereditary, for his family comes from Sparta. He is currently applying his scientific training to provide new insights into hoplite combat at www.hollow-lakedaimon.blogspot.com. He is indebted to Russian hooligans, whose tireless shenanigans allow us to witness the fluidity and spontaneous order that arises in crowds of belligerent men.

Further reading

- J.K. Anderson, *Military theory and practice in the age of Xenophon*. Berkeley and Los Angeles 1970.
- P. Bardunias, 'The *aspis*. Surviving Hoplite Battle', in: *Ancient Warfare* I.3 (2007), 11-14.
- G.L. Cawkwell, 'Orthodoxy and Hoplites', in: *The Classical Quarterly* 39 (1989), 375-389.
- P. Connolly, D. Sim, and C. Watson, 'An Evaluation of the Effectiveness of Three Methods of Spear Grip Used In Antiquity', in: *Journal of Battlefield Technology*, Vol. 4.2 (2001).
- A.K. Goldsworthy, 'The *Othismos*, Myths and Heresies: The Nature of Hoplite Battle', in: *War and History* 4 (1997), 1-26.
- V.D. Hanson, *The Western Way of War*. Oxford 1989.
- V.D. Hanson (ed.), *Hoplites. The Classical Greek Battle Experience*. London and New York 1991.
- P. Krentz, 'The Nature of Hoplite Battle', in: *Classical Antiquity* 16 (1985), 50-61.
- P. Krentz, 'Continuing the *othismos* on the *othismos*', in: *Ancient History Bulletin* 8 (1994), 45-9.
- P. Krentz, D. Kagan and D. Showalter, *The Battle of Marathon*. New Haven 2010.
- R.D. Luginbill, '*Othismos*: the importance of the mass-shove in hoplite warfare', in: *Phoenix* 48 (1994), 51-61.
- L. B. Perkins, *Crowd Safety and Survival*. Lulu.com, 2005.
- A. Schwartz, *Reinstating the Hoplite: Arm, Armor, and Phalanx Fighting in Archaic and Classical Greece*. Stuttgart 2010.
- H. van Wees, *Greek Warfare. Myths and Realities*. London 2004.

Dress and equipment of the Greek forces
A craze for scales

Over the Archaic Period infantry had emerged as the predominant force on the Greek battlefield. This was the case for predominantly financial reasons. The state did not have the financial means at its disposal to fund other arms of service. We do hear of states which supported forces of cavalry even as far back as the Archaic period, such as Macedonia, Thessaly or Boeotia, but these are very much exceptions. The state had to find the means of compensat- ing a cavalryman for the loss of his horse in battle, and recompense him for his outlay on fodder, and this was beyond the means of the typi- cal Greek (city-) state at this time, and for a long time to come. Furthermore, in order for specialist infantry, such as archers, to be prop- erly trained, the state had to recompense such indi- viduals for their time taken off work to develop their military skills.

By Nicholas Sekunda

The typical Greek city-state during the Archaic period did not possess any permanent income, and the citizenry could hardly be expected to vote for taxation of themselves except under the most exceptional of circumstances. Therefore the typical Greek army during the Archaic period consisted of citizen-soldiers, serving as infantrymen at their own cost, and providing their own equipment

The hoplite spear
The ancient Greeks called this type of infantrymen *hoplites*, literally "man-at-arms" after the arms and armour that he carried. The principal offensive weapon of the hoplite was his spear. In his play *The Persians* Aeschylus, who fought at Marathon, portrays the Persian Wars as a contest between the oriental bow and the Greek spear. The latter was slightly above a man's height and made of ash. Homer refers to ashen spears (*Iliad* 5.66, 19.390, 22.225) as does Tyrtaios (fragment 19.13). The reasons for this are explained by Pliny in his *Natural History* (16.84[228]) "Ash is the most compliant of wood in work of any kind. And is better than hazel for spears, lighter than cornel, and more pliable than sorb." Other woods might be

Very well preserved example of a late-type Corinthian helmet. The small hole in the brow perhaps indicates the helmet was captured and nailed to a temple wall as a trophy. About 500 BC, now in the Archaeological Museum, Munich, Germany.

© *Karwansaray Publishers*

© Nicholas Sekunda

This detail from the Oxford Brygos cup (see p.86) shows two hoplites arming themselves. A young man in a chitoniskos *tunic clips on his greaves. To the right a fully-armed hoplite looks to the rear; his shield-blazon is a bull. One of the labours of Herakles was to hunt down the Marathonian bull, and in the conventions of Greek vase-painting the shield-device of a bull, or a bull's head, indentified an individual as a 'Marathon-fighter'. At his feet lies the ear of a bow, perhaps an enigmatic reference to the absence of archers from the battle of Marathon.*

stronger, but ash was chosen as it combined great strength with light weight, mainly due to its straight and even grain. Imperfections in the grain would be eradicated during the process of preparing the shaft for use.

A tree would be felled in mid-winter, when there was the least amount of sap in it. The process of seasoning depends on the sap drying out of the wood, and during this time internal splits could develop in the trunk. The trunk would be split into progressively smaller sections with a hammer and wedges to eradicate these potential sources of weakness, until a billet of suitable thickness was arrived at. The billet was then rounded into shape with a spoke-shave, called a *xuele*. In ancient Greece there was a distinct profession of "spear-whittler" (*doruxoos*) who worked in a "spear-whittlery" (*doruxeion*). Plutarch (*Life of Pelopidas* 12.1) mentions that in the liberation of Thebes in 379 BC, the insurgents armed themselves with weapons taken from the workshops of the 'spear-whittlers' and sword-makers in the

city. Finally, the shaft was fitted with a spear-head and butt-spike.

Spear-heads, usually of iron rather than bronze, could be of different shapes, but generally tended to be leaf-shaped. The bronze spear-butt was called a *styrax* or *sauroter* ("lizard-slayer"). Towards the end of the Archaic period they tended to be of a standard shape: a hollow cylinder for a third of their length to accommodate the spear-shaft, and, after a connecting ring, were generally square in section for the remaining two-thirds, tapering towards the tip. The spear-butt served principally to fix the spear upright in the ground when not in use. Spear-heads and butts were fixed in place by means of hot pitch. Spear-shafts tapered somewhat towards the tip, and due to the weight of the butt-spike the centre of balance fell at about one third of the length from the butt. A hand-grip could be fitted by binding a leather thong onto the shaft.

The spear was by far the most important weapon of the Greek hoplite. The sword was only used as a weapon of last

resort. Other hoplite equipment was more subject to regional variation. The Greek army that fought at Marathon was exclusively Athenian, though reinforced by a contingent of Plataeans. What follows applies to military equipment as attested on Athenian vase paintings.

The composite cuirass

From the middle of the sixth century the composite cuirass completely replaced the bronze plate 'bell' cuirass at Athens. Bronze plate cuirasses, in their later form – the 'muscle-cuirass' only regained their popularity at Athens in the 460s. The main body of the composite cuirass normally consisted of four hinged plates wrapped round the trunk and secured in place on the left side at the front. A chest-plate, apparently separate, was added later, and the shoulder-guards brought down from the back and tied down at the front. The groin was protected by a double row of groin-flaps attached to the trunk-plates of the cuirass.

The material from which the plates of the composite cuirass were made is not known for certain, because no example of a composite cuirass has survived intact from this period. The first intact example was discovered in 1977 in the tomb probably belonging to Philip II of Macedon. This example was constructed of iron plates, but the plates in earlier examples might have been constructed of a wider range of materials, such as hardened leather or linen (See also the debate in *Ancient Warfare* IV.3).

Plates of scale armour start to be depicted at the end of the sixth century on Attic vases showing composite cuirasses. A fragment of bronze scale armour of unknown date, seemingly originally silver plated, has been found at Olympia, and two sets of alternating bronze and iron scales fixed to a thin bronze backing, the largest about 8cm across at, Delphi, in an archaeological context dating from the early seventh century to the late fifth century. These fragments confirm the evidence of the vase-paintings.

At the same date, areas of lozenge-shaped patterns start to be shown on the surface areas of the plates which made up the composite cuirass. It would be logical to conclude that this style of surface decoration was inspired by the pattern of the scales.

Helmet types

The Corinthian helmet continued to be popular among the Athenians, along-side a new type, the 'Chalcidian'. This new type is christened from the Chalcidian vases dating to the late sixth century on which they are first depicted. These vases, it is now known, were produced in southern Italy, and the earliest actual examples of the helmet come from Chalcis (Euboea, Greece) and south Italy. The Chalcidian type differs from the Corinthian in having cut-outs for the ears and rounded cheek-pieces. Within a short time of its first appearance the cheek-pieces of the Chalcidian helmet were hinged, allowing them to be worn in the upright position. Thus the this type of helmet was at once more comfortable to wear than the Corinthian helmet, and afforded the wearer an increased field of vision and improved hearing.

Modern scholarship continues to distinguish between Chalcidian helmets and 'Attic' ones. Like Everson (2004) I consider that the Attic helmet "is really just another Chalcidian variation" and there is no essential difference between the two types. The Attic helmet is only attested in representations, above all in vase paintings, where it appears with a more pronounced curve to the neck-guard, long forward-curving

One of a pair of greaves, found together with the helmet of their owner in his grave, a warrior called Dendas. Made in Greek workshops in Magna Graecia, southern Italy, around 500 BC. Now in the Archaeological Museum, Munich, Germany.

cheek-pieces which are not rounded, and no nose-guard. Preserved examples of the Chalcidian helmet invariably have a small nasal. These small differences could all conceivably be due to artistic shortcomings.

It was previously believed that bronze was exclusively used in the production of Greek helmets, but it is now known that iron too was used in the production of a certain number of the component parts of the helmet.

Greek armourers started to experiment with the use of scales, presumably of iron, in helmet production too. This is evident from Attic vase-paintings of this period. A further type of helmet is shown on a number of Attic vases of this period as well. In these representations a number of light-coloured studs or rings appear against a dark background on the skull of the helmet. Everson (2004) has suggested that these designs would have been painted onto the helmet, without reflecting in any way the method of construction. I have previously tried to explain this feature as a way of depicting the outside appearance of helmets made up of iron plates, riveted together. The outside of helmets constructed in this way would have been covered on the outside with material or leather to stop the iron plates from rusting, but the rivets would be revealed on the outside.

The hoplite shield

The principal defensive weapon of the hoplite was his shield, and it was around the turn of the fifth century that we detect a fundamental change in the hoplite shield. Before the end of the sixth century BC the hoplite shield had been made from a number of planks of wood glued together and then turned on a lathe. Only the rim was reinforced with a bronze covering. From about the beginning of the fifth century the Greeks developed the technique to cover the entire outer surface with a thin bronze sheet. To this day we do not understand how this was possible with the technology then available to the Greeks. Greek armourers seem to have also experimented with scales in the construction of hoplite shields, to judge from the evidence of Attic vase-paintings, and the surfaces of other shields appear decorated with lozenge patterns too, reflecting these experiments.

© Dariusz Bufnal

Plate one: Ready for battle

The figures in this plate are all based on Greek warriors shown on the Oxford Brygos Cup (see also page 86).

LEFT: The bronze helmet is of the conventional Chalcidian or Attic type, but the composite cuirass is anything but conventional. The shoulder-guards appear standard enough, but the trunk-plates are decorated with vertical and horizontal lines dividing the cuirass into small squares, and one wonders if this is a way of portraying another style of Greek armour in use at the time. The lines could represent lines of surface stitching, holding in place small square plates of iron or bronze; the Ancient Greek equivalent of a medieval brigantine in effect. The rectangular decoration is certainly very unusual, though not unique.

of iron plates riveted together and then covered on the outside with some kind of material or leather. The rivet-heads are, however, plainly visible on the outside. In the example shown here, the other helmet components are shown as iron. Otherwise the helmet is of a quite conventional shape, of the Chalcidian/Attic type. Again, the helmet is worn with the cheek-flaps up.

The figure has his back to us, and the shoulder-guard assembly is clearly of scale construction, presumably iron. The scales are left exposed on the surface, and it is very noticeable that the scales are oriented upwards, not downwards. It was evidently considered more important that the scales should run downwards at the front, thus affording more protection from downward blows to the shoulder from the front. Unusually large groin-flaps hang beneath the trunk of the cuirass.

RIGHT: The bronze helmet is again of the Chalcidian/Attic type, and the cheek-flaps are again worn upwards for comfort. An unusual feature of the side-plates and the shoulder-guards of the cuirass is that the surface is decorated in a diamond-shape pattern. This is a frequently found feature found at the beginning of the fifth century, and could reflect the new internal construction method from iron scales then so much in vogue.

© Nicholas Sekunda

The interior 'tondo' of the Oxford Brygos cup shows two middle-aged, bearded warriors rising from a common tomb. They stand back-to-back, un-sheathing their swords for action. Presumably these two heroes are the only two officers who died, the Polemarch Callimachus and the stratēgos *Stesilaus, who as Heodotus (6.114) says, fell in the fighting near the ships. Note the scales on the side-plates and the groin-flaps on the composite cuirass worn by the figure on the right.*

The archaeological evidence, especially from Olympia, shows that from the beginning of the fifth century greaves had begun to be decorated in a style purely representing the human anatomy, without any stylistic decoration, and they had lost their internal lining, with its accompanying lines of tiny holes to bind the lining in place.

CENTRE: The helmet is of 'composite' construction, although in this example no iron scales are visible on the surface. The helmet rather seems to be composed

© Dariusz Bufnal

Plate two: Arming the hoplite

LEFT: This figure is un-bearded and is obviously young. He is wearing a light type of linen tunic, called *chitoniskos* according to the conventions of Greek art history and archaeology. This garment was particularly popular at the turn of the sixth century, and is very often shown, as in this case, as being worn under armour. It is shown as very crinkly, as befits a fine linen

garment, and is worn very baggy, and very loose under the arms, gathered in sharp folds below the waist belt. Xenophon (*Anabasis* 3.2.7) tells us that he wore his finest clothes for battle. One might have expected the *chitoniskos* to be dyed in bright colours, but it might have also been the standard practice to wear fine linen tunic bleached plain white in this period.

The warrior is shown clipping his high-

ly elastic (on account of their thinness) bronze greaves into place on his lower legs. This was the normal sequence when arming. The cuirass inhibited bending the trunk of the body, and made it difficult to bend down sufficiently to put the greaves on afterwards.

He has already perched a Corinthian helmet on the top of his head. The Corinthian helmet gave better protection

in this plate. He is shown putting on his composite cuirass over his *chitoniskos*. In this example the composite cuirass fastens at the front (in other examples the front-plate is in one piece). The two-piece front-plate of the cuirass is composed of small bronze scales sewn onto a stiffened leather base.

The shoulder-guard assembly shown in this representation is probably composed of three separate plates; the principal one of the whole shoulder-guard assembly being made of small bronze scales sewn onto leather. In this representation, the shoulder-guards have not yet been tied down in place, and so the complete shoulder-guard assembly is shown from the back. A second piece of stiffened leather was probably glued onto the back of the first piece. Onto this backing the bronze scales were sewn, and the whole plate was held together with a further piece of leather wrapped around the edge. The main plate protected both shoulders at the back. Two rectangular extensions of this main plate projected to either side of the head. In between these two shoulder projections was a single shorter extension to protect the nape of the neck. The two shoulder extensions terminate in two additional smaller plates, which were probably attached by means of small hinges. These two attached plates run flush with the inside edge of the shoulder plate, but their outside edge does not extend as far as the outside edge of either shoulder extension. This feature was designed to allow more freedom of movement to the arms. On other representations of the composite cuirass the shoulder-guards seem to be constructed in one piece.

At a later stage in the arming process the two shoulder extensions would be wrapped over either shoulder, and tied in place by a leather thong attached to the inside of the attached plate. When the composite cuirass had been tied together at the front, an additional plate to protect the chest would be attached above the front plate. It was to this chest-plate that the two thongs of the two projecting extensions of the shoulder-guard would be tied, either by means of small rings, or of matching thongs, attached to the chest-plate. The exact method is unclear from existing representations.

Attached below the two-piece front-plate, a double row of groin-flaps is shown, one below the other. The inside

to the wearer than most other types, but it gave restricted vision from the eye-holes, and severely hampered hearing. Therefore, he wears it on top of his head for the time being. He will adjust it to its correct position immediately before battle. Along the top of the hoplite's helmet he wears a crest, made of horsehair, which might have been brightly dyed. It is fitted into a crest-holder, typically decorated

at this period with two lines of squares, in alternating light and dark colours. The crest-holder was held in place on the helmet by a system of clasps, soldered onto the helmet, which allowed the crest to be detached when the helmet was not in use, or being cleaned.

CENTRE: The figure wears a beard, and so is older than the other two figures shown row is slightly lower than the outside row, and is staggered in relation to the outside row, the inside row being designed to cover the gaps in the outside row. From representational evidence, it is clear that the groin-flaps were usually permanently attached to the principal plates guarding the trunk. In this example, the groin flaps seem to be constructed from layers of hardened leather glued together, but it is possible that metal plates reinforced the construction. In other representations, the groin-flaps are clearly shown to be constructed of metal scales sewn onto a leather base.

The shield is shown propped up against the body of the figure in the centre, and his helmet sitting on the ground behind him. In this case, the helmet is of composite construction even if it is of a design and shape that has been labelled 'Chalcidian' or 'Attic'; there is no substantive difference between the two types. The bowl of the helmet is of scale construction, attached to a single rim incorporating the visor and neck-guard. A pair of cheek-guards are attached to this piece by hinges. These hinges allowed the cheek-pieces to be positioned upright even when the helmet was being worn, affording unre-

© Courtesy François Lissarrague

This representation confirms the use of metal scales even for the production of shields: in this case of 'Boeotian' type, and so in all probability mythological. Pottier interpreted the scene as showing a 'trophée d'armes', but the first trophy was erected at Marathon, and many years after at that as part of the campaign to glorify the reputation of his father carried out by the Athenian politician Kimon. It more probably represents the arms of Achilles.

stricted vision and additional comfort to the wearer until the last minute.

RIGHT: The arming process is virtually complete now. The subject has put on his chest-plate, and tied down his shoulder-guards. The chest-plate is not rectangular, but extends further upwards in the centre, affording protection for the throat, but is lower at the two edges, affording additional mobility to the shoulders and upper arms. He is shown slinging his sword on his left. In this case the *chitoniskos* is shown as crinkly throughout its whole length, and not gathered in sharp folds below the waist belt. This slight variation is probably to be explained by the vagaries of fashion at the end of the Archaic period. ●

Nicholas Sekunda has published many books and articles about warfare and warriors of the Ancient world. He currently teaches at the Institute of Archaeology, Gdansk, Poland.

© Vienna, Kunsthistoriches Museum 3694

The career of Douris, a rare vase-painter whose real name is known to us, stretched from about 500 to nearly 460 BC. This is an early cup decorated by him – it has his signature – and so dates to roughly the time of Marathon. The subject is mythological, showing the departure of the 'Seven Against Thebes'. It is of extreme interest, because it not only documents the current craze for scale armour, but depicts the various stages in arming oneself the Greek hoplite went through. At the end of the Archaic period it was still popular to wear one's hair long. All three figures wear a head-band, although it is most visible on the figure on the left. The head-band held down the hair in front of the brow, ensuring that it did not obscure the vision of the warrior, and gathered the hair together in a bun at the back

Further reading

- T. Everson, *Warfare in Ancient Greece. Arms and Armour from the Heroes of Homer to Alexander the Great.* Stroud 2004.
- E. Jarva, *Archaiologia on Archaic Greek Body Armour* (=Studia Archaeologica Septentrionalia 3. Rovaniemi 1995).
- A. Snodgrass, *Early Greek Armour and Weapons from the end of the Bronze Age to 600 b.c* Edinburgh 1964.

The Achaemenid army at Marathon

The army of all nations

For the Persians the military campaign of 490 BC was a continuation of their policy of expansion which had been implemented almost from the beginning of Darius' reign. They had started with the Aegean islands, taking Samos and after that the northern Balkans. The King of Kings commanded an expedition into Scythian territory in 513, crossing the Lower Danube and reaching the general area of modern Moldova and southern Ukraine. In 512, his general Megabysos conquered the southern Thracian tribes and the Paionians neighboring with them to the west. The Macedonian king Amyntas I recognized the more or less nominal authority of the Persians too. Megabysos' successor in command of troops in western Asia Minor, Otanes son of Sisamnes, one of the six conspirators associated with Darius in the overthrowing of Gaumata, continued the occupation of islands in the Aegean, taking Lemnos and Imbros, as well as the Byzantium on the continent.

By Marek Wozniak

Conquests and punitive expeditions to Europe started again following the suppression by the Persians of an Ionian rebellion on the coasts of Asia Minor and Cyprus in 500-493 BC. At this time the Persians took Chios, Lesbos and Tenedos. Another less successful campaign conducted by Mardonius son of Gobryas in Thrace in 493 dampened the Persians keenness to conquer the north. Mardonius managed to take Thasos, confirm the Persian hitherto rather nominal authority over Macedonia and defeat the Thracians in heavy border fighting, but he also lost half his fleet to bad weather around the Athos peninsula. Darius replaced Mardonius with Datis, whom Herodotus considered to be a Mede by origin, and Artaphernes the Younger, son of Artaphernes the Older, *satrap* of Lydia. The expedition these two were to lead was to follow the sea route through Rhodes, Samos along the Cyclades, where the Persians had conquered Naxos and most likely Paros, all the way to Euboea and later Attica: straight into the heart of continental Hellas.

Commanders

Little is known of the commanders of this campaign. To believe Herodotus they could have been of equal rank. This would fit in well with the practice of power diversification common in the Persian court and administration.

Datis appears to have been older and much more experienced than Artafernes. One of the records from the archive in Persepolis suggests that in the winter of 495/494 the King of Kings had requested him to supervise, in person, the preparations for the ultimate military campaign against the Ionians. It means that he must have been acquainted with the Greeks and their battle tactics. He was also *satrap* of the strategic and politically important province of Media hence he should have been an expert cavalry tactician.

As for Artafernes, his nomination derived from the position of his father, Artaphernes the Elder, brother to Darius and *satrap* of the most important of the Asia Minor provinces. Interestingly, Herodotus concentrates more on Artaphernes than on Datis when describing their taking of command. Datis may have been the more experienced of the two and was surely in charge of command in the field, as indicated by mentions of his actions during the fighting for individual islands (and hardly surprising, if the army included a large, possibly Medes and Saka, cavalry contingent), but the young, well-born Artaphernes with good standing at the court could very well have had nominal command. Pausanias' mention of the mangers of Artafernes' horses (without a word about Datis) can be construed as further proof. Artafernes would have been the royal court's general in command. His career in the Persian army and administration was not interrupted by the campaign and in 480, possibly already as *satrap* of Lydia in place of his father, he appeared at the head of the Lydian contingent in the campaign launched by Xerxes against the Greeks. Governors of this important province were men of wealth, had a fair amount of independence and huge influence in the Persian empire. Such was their importance and independence that we find a dangerous trend, started by Oroites who ruled his *satrapy* like an independent lord, and even rebelled against Darius I.

The invasion army

Sailing from island to island, the Persian armada of 600 ships (including an unknown number of special barges for transporting horses) conquered town after town, enslaving large numbers of local inhabitants. Karystos in southern Euboea was the first goal. There the Persians organized a camp for expeditions against Eretria and Athens. The bay was an excellent choice from the strategic point of view: big enough for several ships, open to the south, hence sheltering the fleet from northern winds and dangerous currents which had always haunted the Persian fleet in the Aegean. Moreover, it was at approximately the same distance from Eretria to the northwest and Athens to the west.

The armada commanded by Artaphernes and Datis can be analyzed in terms of the number of warships and their load-bearing kind to give an idea of the approximate size of the Persian army. Classical Greek sources gave the number of Achaemenid dead in battle, but had little idea of the actual force that attacked the Greeks; over time there was a tendency to overestimate Persian manpower beyond all proportions.

Writing after the Marathon campaign, Herodotus wisely limited himself to mentioning just 600 triremes carrying troops. It seems that he does not include in this number the barges constructed specially for the transport of horses for the invasion army, perhaps for the first time in history. Nothing is said about the number of these barges. In a fragment indirectly referring to the Battle of Marathon, Herodotus notes that the Athenians defeated 46 peoples of the Persian Empire, but this number refers to the contingents which he describes in Xerxes' huge army of 480 BC. It is more than likely that 46 corresponds to the number of known peoples in the Achaemenid Empire and hence is questionable also with regard to the royal army of Xerxes, let alone the expeditionary forces of Artaphernes and Datis.

Despite Herodotus' restraint, other writers speculated on the size of the Persian army at Marathon. In an epigram about the battle, Simonides, a near contemporary of Herodotus, gave the invading army at 90,000. Since the work was commissioned by the Athenians, the exaggeration was justified as a propagandist device. But the numbers grew. Nepos writes of 200,000 Achaemenid soldiers commanded by Artaphernes and Datis (of which 100,000 went to battle) and 10,000 cavalry (!). The fleet counted 500 ships, which is actually very likely and if the number referred to troop ships alone, it would correspond roughly to Herodotus' information. Plutarch gave the army of Artaphernes and Datis already at 300,000. The same number was quoted by Pausanias and by the Byzantine lexicon *Suda*. In *Menexenos*, Plato estimated the Achaemenid expeditionary corps at 500,000; Justin raised it again and set it at 600,000. The size of the battlefield, not to

mention ordinary logistics, is sufficient to demonstrate the complete incredibility of these numbers.

Clearly, the accounts of Herodotus and Nepos are the only reasonably secure assumptions for estimating Persian troops. Describing Xerxes' fleet invading Greece, Herodotus reported each trireme as carrying soldiers and equipment beside the oarsmen. The ships were supplied by subordinate peoples, like the Phoenicians, Ionians, Cypriots, etc., who more than likely manned these vessels as well. The crews had to be highly skilled and prepared to maneuver precisely in the heat of battle. A full load encompassed 170 oarsmen and 30 soldiers. Ships intended for troop transport rather than battle could have had fewer oarsmen, which could be redistributed to a lesser number of ships if a battle situation arose. It also seems, considering Persian action in the Aegean and what Herodotus reports the orders were for Artaphernes and Datis, that apart from territorial conquests, the Achaemenids were interested in taking as many captives as possible. Therefore, they needed space on their ships for this human cargo. It can be assumed that one trireme carried between 30 and 40 soldiers. The same number was given for the fleet of Chios at Lade. Thus, assuming the Persian fleet counted 600 ships, including 500 triremes for the infantry the infantry numbers can stand at 15,000-20,000 men. Modern scholarship has reached similar conclusions, opting however for the higher number. Nick Sekunda in his work on the Marathon battle has observed that the general number of soldiers would have had to reflect the system of tens command in the Achaemenid army, at least in key units. Consequently, the army could have been 20,000 strong, being composed of two *baivarabam* units of 10,000 soldiers each.

As for the cavalry, their participation in the campaign was noted by Herodotus and Nepos after him, but none of the available sources even hints at the presence of cavalry units at Marathon. Cavalry was virtually nonexistent in the armies of the Greek poleis in the beginning of the 5th century, hence Persian domination in this sphere required little effort. A thousand Thessalian riders easily defeated Athenian troops in 511 BC. The Greeks were well aware of this. If the remaining 100 ships were used to carry horses and

their riders, and each ship carried about 20 horses (during the Sicilian expedition the Athenians sent one ship with 30 horses as part of the expeditionary force), then the cavalry counted some 2000 riders, an enormous force by Hellenic standards.

Of the numerous national contingents making up the Great King's army, Herodotus lists only the Persians and Saka as taking part in the battle of Marathon. The presence of other divisions should be surmised, however, from the fact that he labels only these two groups at the center of the line. Having received the command and their orders straight from Darius (it was the summer, so it must have been in Ecbatana) Artaphernes and Datis moved to Cilicia where they were supposed to embark, collecting on the way divisions alerted for the campaign by royal order. According to Plutarch and the *Suda* lexicon, Datis was supposed to be a *satrap*, of Media perhaps, which gave him the privilege of having his own guard organized along the lines of the royal one. In the case of Persian nobles, this guard was drafted, like the royal guard, from among native Persians, military settlers inhabiting a given province. But according to Herodotus and Diodorus, Datis was a Mede by origin. His guard could thus have been composed of Medes (although Darius may not have tolerated nationalism to this degree). Persians forming the infantry core of the invading army could have been drafted for the campaign (much like the soldiers of Otanes in Xerxes' army, from among settlers placed by special royal order under the command of specially appointed officers.

Warriors from the Scythian tribes whom the Persians called *Sakai* must have constituted a similar case. A deeply assimilated Scythian diaspora had inhabited northern Media from the 7th century. Saka settlers were also settled in the Achaemenid period in provinces like Babylonia, their obligation being to supply soldiers for the armies of the king and satrap. Many Saka enlisted in the army of the King of Kings as highly skilled mercenaries. They originated mainly from the two nomadic tribes living in the steppe around the Caspian and Aral seas and are mentioned in Classical and Persian sources (so-called Saka Haumavarka, also called Amyrgian Sakai living nearer to the borders of the Achaemenid Empire, and the Saka Tigrakhauda, presumably situ-

…

Satrap's guard

Based on a description of the march of Xerxes' personal guard during the expedition to Greece and an analysis of monumental reliefs from the palace complex in Persepolis, it can be surmised that the royal guard (copied by the *satraps*) formed two one-thousand-strong elitist infantry units (royal shield-bearers called *arštibara* in Persian or *doriphoroi* in Greek, and sometimes, from the shape of the spear-butts, *melophoroi*, "apple-bearers"), and a detachment of guard veterans occasionally referred to as the "royal archers". They had colorful uniforms, while the spear-butts of their weapons were the same as those of the officers of the 'Immortal' guards.

Detail of one of the reliefs from the palace of Darius I at Susa, showing the pomegranate-shaped spear-butt, similar to the round, apple-shaped spear-butts of other guardsmen.

ated farther out). A large Saka contingent had fought already for Cyrus II in the war against the Masagetai. Artaphernes and Datis must have had such allies (or mercenaries) in their army.

The Saka were famous as cavalrymen, but they, like the Masagetai, they also supplied infantry. It thus comes as no surprise that in the early Achaemenid period especially, when Iranian-speaking tribes formed the core of the assault forces, the Persians, contrary to some modern scholarship which opts for Persian-style cavalry at Marathon, drafted Saka warriors for both key formations in their army. Their mercenary character, as well as their combat skills, turned the Saka into a real menace. Their cavalry proved extremely courageous and effective at Plataea as was their infantry at Marathon.

The army of Datis and Artaphernes must have been composed of other divisions besides the two labeled *expressis verbis*. Assuming Datis was indeed satrap of Media, he would not have foregone on calling on the well-reputed Medes soldiers. In the Achaemenid military tradition a satrap personally commanded troops from his province. The Medes, like the Saka, had both cavalry and infantry units. Like the Persians, Kissians/Elamites and Hyrcanians (possibly also Ionians, Lydians

and Mesopotamian peoples), the Medes produced heavily armed infantry units, without which it would be difficult to imagine any bigger military campaign.

The commanders' route from Media to Cilicia led through northern Mesopotamia, hence it is not impossible that at the King's order the invasion army was joined by units of local settlers. Indirect evidence of their participation was produced by the bronze conical helmet found at Olympia and identified as a votive offering from the Marathon battlefield by its inscription "To Zeus from the Athenians who took it from the Medes". The helmet type in the shape of a bulging cone was in common use in northern Mesopotamia (in the Assyrian army) and eastern Asia Minor, occurring only sporadically elsewhere. Kubanian type helmets, originating presumably from Elam, were much more popular in Achaemenid Iran and in Scythian territory, that is, Kuban, perhaps a result of contact with Iranian peoples. The helmet from Olympia is slightly different from examples depicted in Assyrian reliefs and actual finds. Its shape and construction, however, made out of a single piece of bronze, suggest that it derived from an old tradition of Mesopotamian helmets.

Cilicia was the rallying point for all the troops. The last camp before ship-

ping out stood in the Aleian Plain. The ruler of Cilicia, Syennesis, considered like the Carian rulers a confederate of the Persians, opened the port and may have supplied at least part of the transport ships. Lydian soldiers may have also joined the army considering that Artaphernes was the son of the Lydian satrap. This people had gained renown already a couple of generations earlier for the armored infantry patterned after the Greeks and excellent heavy cavalry. As for the Ionians, the recently put-down revolt could not have engendered the Great King's trust and they do not appear to have played any significant role in any of the fighting during this campaign. But they seem to have participated in some way, perhaps as oarsmen on ships supplied by the Ionian cities, because they managed, in the night before the battle, to inform the Athenians that the Persian cavalry had been withdrawn.

If the army of Artaphernes and Datis reflected the makeup described above based on indirect evidence, then it was a small force, but made up of troops of the highest fighting mettle and experience.

Weaponry and equipment
The light character of the Achaemenid army appears to be a suggestion adopted

© Karwansaray Publishers

Alabastron - a container for massage oils and perfumes - showing a Scythian archer. Around 500 BC, now in the Pergamon Museum, Berlin.

from Herodotus who described in book seven of his *Histories* the "shockingly colorful" and exotic national divisions and commented on the weaponry of Mardonios' soldiers at Plataea. A look at images of Persian, Medes, Saka and Kissian soldiers in Hellenic art and a careful perusal of descriptions of weaponry and equipment of the Iranian-speaking units which led the field in the Achaemenid army, coupled with an examination of archaeological finds of armor from, for example, Persepolis, Deve Hŭyŭk, Pasargadae, Sardis, Memphis etc., produces an entirely different picture.

The Persian division was the most battle-worthy in the army of Datis and Artafernes. Neither Herodotus nor any other source give any numbers, but if it is assumed that Datis' satrapal guard was formed of Persians, they could have numbered according to different estimates

from 1000 to 2000. The fact that they stood at the center of the line could be proof of their guard, or elite character (as many sources confirm that the commander-in-chief and the elite units with him ordinarily occupied this position).

The only certain depictions of select Persian infantrymen from the times of Darius are found on reliefs decorating the royal palaces at Susa and Persepolis. We can see spear-bearers and archers holding spears with leaf-shaped points and spear-butts in the form of stylized apples and pomegranates mounting on the shafts. The Persepolis reliefs suggest that each such division had shield-bearers (equipped with spears and tall rectangular shields), and archers. These shields, called *sparā* or *gerron* in Greek, were made of rectangular pieces of raw leather reinforced with hard Asiatic reeds needled through specially cut holes in closely set vertical lines. The drying leather contracted, creating a highly resilient but light shield. The upper and lower edges were additionally reinforced with leather trimming, on the inside a single vertical handle was mounted. These shields could be as high as 1.5 m and from 0.60 to 0.80 m wide. Characteristic patterns on the surface of these shields are well rendered in Greek vase painting. The archaeological record unfortunately has not produced any shield-boards from the Achaemenid period, but there are three examples of almost identical shields from 3rd century AD contexts in Dura Europos. The two better preserved ones can be seen in the Damascus museum, the third in New Haven, Connecticut.

These huge *sparā* were in use in the times of Darius as well, both by the guard and by regular shield-bearers. Wooden shields of the Dipylon or Boetian type were introduced in the reign of Xerxes, a fact noted in the reliefs from the Throne Hall in Persepolis. Ordinary infantry line units during the Marathon campaign still

used the *sparā*, but much smaller in size than the shields of the guards and shield-bearers.

The spears of the soldiers from the first five rows of their unit, who were called the Argyraspides ("Silver Shields") by the 3rd century AD philosopher Iamblichos, were rather short and massive, approximately 2-2.5 m long. Images from audience reliefs in the Treasury at Persepolis and from the gates of the lateral entrances to the portico of Darius' I Tačara show that the spears of the royal guard from the last rows of a unit could have been up to 3.5 m long. The five last rows of *melophoroi* were not equipped with shields intentionally so that they could use their spears two-handed, as in hunting. According to Xenophon, an extremely hard, but resilient and elastic wood from the cornel tree was used in Persia to make spear shafts for the cavalry (identical to those for the infantry). In this period the metal points still had very long sockets (see the palace frieze from Susa) and wide sharp blades, still suggestive of Elamite influence.

Shield-bearers from the guard units were also equipped with long, heavy swords resembling the Roman *gladius* of the Imperial period. An example of such a sword, which derived like many other elements of the arms of Persian infantrymen from Elamite models (similar swords are featured among the "Luristan bronzes", and probably are visible on the Assyrian relief from Assurbanipal palace in Nineveh), was discovered in the barracks of the Royal Guard at Persepolis. The blade, forged from one piece of steel together with the hilt and pommel, was 80 cm long finishing in a long sharp blade tip. Like the Greek *xiphos* and the Roman *gladius*, the Persian sword was designed for thrusting. The length and use in combination with a large rectangular shield also suggests a combat technique resembling what we know of Roman methods. The

Persian scales

Of the 16,000 published scales and fragments of armor from Persepolis only six pieces exceeded 3 cm in any direction (this including two fragments consisting of three scales each), the rest falling within a range of between 1x2 cm and 2x2 cm (including two fragments of armor composed of 12 and about 30 scales respectively). The six scales and armor fragments from Pasargadae all range in length between 2.5 and 2.8 cm, including two fragments, one composed of about 55 scales, the other of about 11 pieces.

Entire sheets of these vividly glazed bricks have been transplanted from the Royal Palace at Susa to both the Louvre in Paris and in the Pergamon Museum in Berlin. The soldiers show are systematically equipped, but vary in the patterns of their clothing as well as their hairstyles.

hilt of the sword from Persepolis had been inlaid with some kind of organic material which decayed or else a priceless inlay that attracted the attention of plundering soldiers of Alexander the Great. The iron itself was left behind.

The mushroom-shaped pommel can be taken as an indication that the described long swords were worn stuck in the belt together with daggers, which are depicted in images of Persian nobles in reliefs from Persepolis (the swords were worn the same way as in Elamite and Mesopotamian models). A statue of King Darius from Susa also features a dagger of this kind, which is stuck in the belt. The wide sleeves of the robes on the guards conceal this detail, but it can be presumed that they also had daggers in their belts.

Soldiers of the royal guard and other guards depicted in reliefs from palaces in Susa, Babylon and Persepolis are shown in court attire, obviously without caps and armor. These can be reconstructed on the grounds of descriptions in Classical sources and images of soldiers in Greek vase painting. Archaeological finds from the Treasury in Persepolis and the Tall-i Taht fort in Pasargadae can also be of use in this respect.

According to Herodotus, all Persian infantrymen (also from the ordinary line units) were still equipped in the times of Xerxes with scale armor that had (...) "iron scales upon them like the scales of a fish". If the ordinary soldiers had such armor, all the more reason that infantrymen from elite troops wore it as well. Herodotus' mention has been confirmed by archaeological finds of isolated scales, armor plates and whole fragments of scale armor from Persepolis and Pasargadae. Their quality

Head of a Persian soldier wearing a Median soft cap or tiara. Now in the Allard Pierson Museum, Amsterdam, the Netherlands.

and perfect execution is best indicated by the size of the scales. These were very small, making the armor extremely elastic. Hellenic representations, such as the most famous Brygos Cup from Oxford and the Bassegio kylix, represented Achaemenid infantry armor (of both shield-bearers and archers) as a kind of vest protecting only the upper body.

The Brygos Cup was painted shortly after the battle and the artist could have used written descriptions as well as images from the times of the conflict showing Persian soldiers, like the wall paintings in the famous *Stoa Poikile*. The ethnicity of the imaged soldiers has been the object of modern debate, even their caps, which are not sufficiently pointed to be identified as Saka (Hellenic painters often depicted all barbarians of Iranian origin in identical manner), were probably

soft Medes tiaras seen in representations of Medes and Persian riders in Persepolis (from the start the Persian cavalry dressed as Medes). Persian infantrymen, as indicated by later representations, adopted at some time (possibly already in the reign of Darius I) the handy Medes caps. Thus, the warriors depicted on the Brygos Cup were either Medes or Persians.

Two of the three Achaemenid soldiers depicted on the cup are shown in cuirasses resembling typical Greek 'linothoraxes' with arm guards in the form of wide flaps extending from the backplate and tied together on the breastplate. The third seems to have a homogenous 'armored vest'. Metal scales (which may also have been shaped differently, as demonstrated by archaeological finds) were expected to cover the entire armor as indicated by the mention in Herodotus, but the armor of the *sparābara* (shield-bearers) on the Brygos Cup is more complicated. Two have the sides covered with scales and a composite front, the smooth surface (in this case ornamented with a painted pattern of diamonds) probably concealing bigger pieces of metal sewn between layers of leather or buckram (stiff cloth, a few pieces of which were discovered at Pasargadae). In one case, probably a double horizontal row of small scales additionally protects the joint between the front plates of a composite armor. The third soldier had armor made entirely of metal scales sewn between layers of leather and kept in place by centrally placed rivets, which recalls medieval brigandines. Another possibility is that this armor had the same construction of breastplate as the other two described above and a backplate in form of simple padded jacket.

All three armors are edged at the bottom by fairly short but wide *pteryges*, vertical straps of leather or buckram protecting the groin and lower abdomen, often decorated with painted ornaments.

The weaponry of Saka infantry did not

differ substantially from that of soldiers representing a much more developed tradition of Elamite, Assyrian and Persian infantry. The front rows were formed of shield-bearers carrying spears and great shields, followed by archers. Saka shown on the platform of the Apadana of Darius in Persepolis had round shields, which were convex and about a meter in diameter. They were made like the later Turkish *kalkans* out of coiled withes (tough, supple twigs) wrapped with thread or leather thongs; a single handle was mounted in the center. Saka shield-bearers used massive and fairly short spears, swords called *akinakes* (copied from the Scythians by other Iranian-speaking peoples as well and used by the Persian cavalry and line infantry too). These swords were worn on the right hip, suspended from a belt attached in a special way to a leaf-like extension of the sheath. The end of the sword, just above the heavy scabbard chape, was tied to the right leg around the knee. This weapon was perfect for combat in a tight shield-bearers' formation. Cavalrymen also used longer swords, sometimes up to a meter in length. Saka warriors also often used battle-axes called *sagaris*.

Since no iconographic depictions of Saka warriors have survived in Greek art, little can be said about their armor. Herodotus did not mention them among the nations using metal armor and only few finds of metal scales have come from Saka territory. Therefore, the Saka shield-bearers may have used light armor made of organic materials (leather, for example) or armor in the form of jackets padded with raw wool, for example. The archers probably did not wear protective armor and nor did most riders who carried nothing but small *sparā* suspended from the left shoulder (a shield of this kind was discovered in tomb I of the Pazyryk necropolis).

Archers from the rear ranks of Persian, Medes and Saka units used (according to Greek vase painting) wide one-sided swords for hand combat; these swords resembled the combat short swords, *kopis*, used by the Greeks. This was a heavy and not very subtle weapon, but lethal when used in a loose formation once the enemy breached the line of shield-bearers. These swords consisted of a blade about 60 cm in length, broadened considerably at the end, and a handle with a characteristic volute instead of a pommel. They were fitted with guards on both or one side of the blade, although there are examples without guard that looked like the famous Gurkha knives (incidentally, images of Gurkhas with a gun in one hand and a *kukhri* knife in the other are an excellent modern parallel for Hellenic representations of Persian archers with swords in one hand and a bow in the other). Achaemenid archers wore either light or no armor at all.

According to Herodotus, Persian and Elamite/Kissian archers used long heavy bows. Many iconographic representations from Susa, Babylon and Persepolis depict archers of the royal guard equipped with long bows slung across the left shoulder. Their length is estimated at 1.5-1.6 m. The bow tips are modeled in the shape of goose heads. Straight grips and their overall size bring them close to Elamite bows, which had been used more than 120 years earlier against the Assyrians. The only difference is the recurve of the limb ends, which the Elamite and Assyrian bows did not have and which was an innovation adopted from the Scythian bow. An example of a Scythian bow, now in the collection of the Museum in Urumchi, comes from the site of Yanghai and is dated to the 7th-6th century BC. The recurve acted like the bow cam in modern hunting bows, significantly increasing the speed of the arrows. The bows of Persian infantry, like the bows of the Scythians and Assyrians, were composite bows, meaning they were glued from a wooden core, horn cover on the backside and prepared sinews on the face side.

The arrows had heavy reed shafts and flat lanceolate iron points about 6 cm long, mounted on the spine. Two such points (plus a third one of bronze with a socket but of almost identical shape) were discovered in the garrison barracks in Persepolis Another ten such arrowheads were found on the battlefield at Thermopylae and one similar to the Persepolis piece with a socket was found at Marathon. The arrows were carried in a long box-like quiver with a flap, slung cross the left shoulder and additionally tied with a strap under the right shoulder.

The Saka, Medes and other eastern Iranian peoples used bows shorter than the Persian bows. Their length ranged between 1 and 1.3 m. The recurve was very strong (the whole bow without the bowstring had the limbs bent into a C-shape).

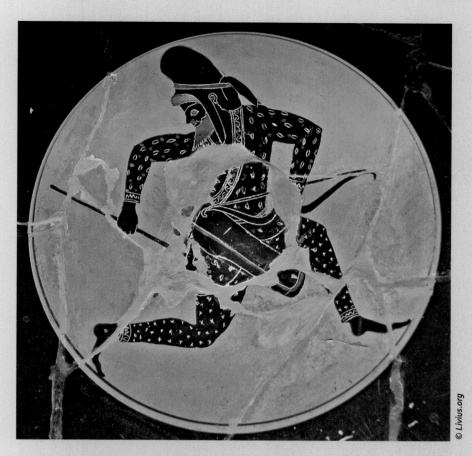

Persian archer preparing his shot holding a battle-axe in one hand and his bow in the other. Similar poses and imagery can be seen on Achaemenid coins. Now in the Louvre, Paris.

© Livius.org

Almost identical examples were discovered in Yanghai and there are dozens of images of them, some in Hellenic art. Bows of this kind were worn suspended from the belt on the left hip in a special case with a pocket/quiver sewn onto the inside (on the outside in combat position facing forward). The part of the bow sticking out of the case was covered with a leather flap to protect the bow from humidity. The arrows used with these bows were much shorter and lighter, fitted with triangular, trilobed points and sometimes fitted with additional hooks on the socket. The small mass of these points resulted in the arrows causing little damage even at high exit velocity, but stuck in the muscle they were very difficult to remove and cutting one out could have caused a substantial bleeding.

The divisions of Iranian-language peoples described above constituted the center of the Persian battle line at Marathon. Unspecified divisions of confederates stood on the flanks (perhaps the heavily armored Lydians on the left flank, for example, covering the retreat to the ships). Shield-bearers stood in front (at least in the Saka-Persian center), protecting archers whose task it was to rain arrows on the approaching enemy for as long as possible. The heavy Persian arrows were definitely capable of penetrating Greek armor. The thousand-man strong guard with the heavily armored shield-bearers positioned itself in front of the commander-in-chief, supported in the back lines by equally heavily armored spear/pike bearers. These select veterans of the Persian infantry were capable of standing up even to the formidable Greek hoplites.

Persians at Marathon

On day 17 of the Athenian month of Metageitnion (11 September 490 BC), the Persian commanders reacted immediately to movements observed in the Hellenic camp on the other, southern side of the plain. They knew that time was running out and they presumably knew of the reinforcements that the Athenians could

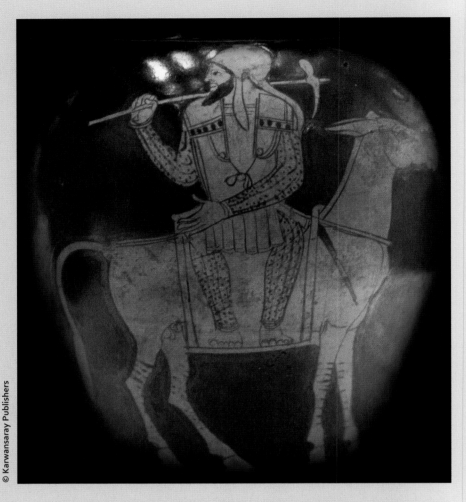

© Karwansaray Publishers

Persian soldier riding a mule, with another - not visible - walking behind him. Note the linothorax-*style body armor and battle-axe. After their victories, the Athenians liked to portray the Persians as peasant weaklings who were defeated due to the Greeks' superior character and political system. Athenian wine-jug, around 470 BC, now in the British Museum, London.*

get from Sparta (Nepos, *Miltiades* 5.4). Accoding to the *Suda* lexicon (supported by many modern scholars), the Persians established contact with the favorably disposed Alkmeonid clan, one of the most powerful Athenian families, and loaded their cavalry onto ships to attack the city from Phaleron and take it in one quick move in the absence of the anti-Persian citizens/hoplites. They were in a difficult situation from a strategic point of view, but that does not mean they were not going to do battle. Their forces were strong enough to let them act successfully on both fronts, although it is true that infantry would have been very useful in pacifying unrest in the occupied town.

It is not known which commander led the mainland troops, but at the first sign of Greek preparations, he spread his troop across the plain from east to west, so that the right flank was based on the Charadra river which in antiquity flowed at the very foot of the Stavrokoraki hill. The Achaemenid line, which was now 1.5 km long and stronger in the center, thus had sufficient space before it to observe the enemy and to rain arrows on attacking soldiers. There were marshes behind the Achaemenids, but there was still room enough for possible maneuvers. The beach with the anchored ships lay to the back of the left flank and this is where the armies were to retreat in case of need. This was the only sensible position from a tactical point of view.

The large numbers of archers which were a standard feature in the Achaemenid army from the start must have had an impact on the Hellenic battle plan.

Speeding up the last part of the attack was supposed to counter this threat. With this in mind, the *strategoi* abandoned the steady approach which was the rule in battles between Greek armies and which ensured cohesion of the line. They ordered the last 200-300 m to be crossed at a run, minimizing the time during which soldiers were exposed to Persian archery fire. Bows of the time had a range from 200 m to 400 m (the heavier the arrows, the greater the resulting force of penetration). As in modern firearms however, the heavier the projectile relative to the applied force, the smaller the effective firing range. Short bows of the Scythian type had the best range (they were used by the Saka and Medes) using light, thin arrows. The shortest range was achieved by the long bows of the Persians with their heavy, almost meter long projectiles which penetrated far further. The use of both types of bows increased the destructiveness of the firepower as the enemy approached. The arrows could not penetrate a hoplite's shield enough to hurt the soldier behind it, but they met with no difficulty in piercing the lighter (non-metallic) armor of Greek infantry.

The Athenian commanders learned that the Persians had embarked their cavalry in the night (Sekunda 2009) and promptly decided to engage the enemy as quickly as possible. Datis and Artaphernes realized that delaying a day could benefit their cause: by giving their soldiers time to attack Athens proper, they could create a situation in which the Spartans, who were coming to aid the Athenians, would find the city conquered and no further battle would be needed. Realizing this possibility, the Greeks not only admitted the necessity to accept battle at Marathon, but they also came to the conclusion that other options were not practical and there was also no time to change the original plan. Reports concerning the line formation assumed by the Greeks on the next day indicated that it was a quadrilateral formation used to counter the threat of an outflanking cavalry attack. The Persians decided to concentrate their thrust in the center and to penetrate enemy lines while keeping the flanks in place.

The standard formation depth in the Achaemenid army was ten rows, while the Greek center was thinner than the usual eight rows and presumably consisted of

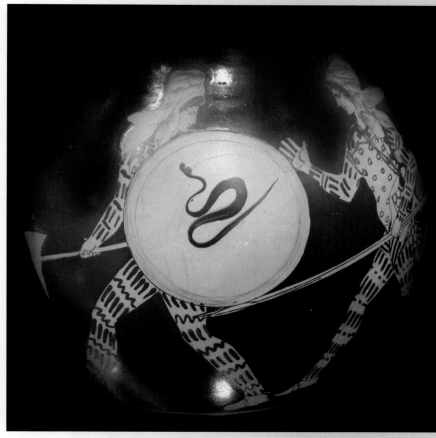

© Karwansaray Publishers

Two Amazons wearing Persian clothing advance into battle. The left-hand Amazon carries a battle-axe and what seems to be an aspis, *while the one on the right is armed with bow and spear. Second half of the fifht century BC, now in the Archaeological Museum, Munich, Germany.*

and cut an evacuation path for themselves. The heavy losses of the forces from the Ajantis *phyle* can be explained, if we assume that the troops were dislocated in this manner and that the battle took the course described above. It was here that Callimachus, *Polemarch* (commander-in-chief) of the Greek forces, was slain as was the strategos *Stesileos*. The Greeks then attacked the beached Persian ships and even took possession of a few nearby ones, but they must have been stopped since the rest of the fleet took on the fleeing Achaemenid soldiers and managed to sail away.

Contrary to what later ancient Greek sources said, the Persian commanders-in-chief survived the battle, as did old Hippias. The losses must have been considerable. The 6,000 dead reported by Herodotus (presumably including those who drowned in the marshes) is a likely number.

For the Greeks and the Athenians in particular, the battle was a memorable event, but for the Persians it was merely a minor drawback which did not affect in any way their plans to conquer Hellas. Just ten years later Xerxes, was back with a huge invasion force, ravaging large expanses of land in northern Greece and torching Athens. Were it not for the death of Darius I in 486 BC, the Achaemenid military giant would have returned much earlier. ●

Marek Wozniak is from Poland and currently working on his PhD thesis, which discusses the Persian Royal Guard.

just four rows of soldiers. The hoplites in the center were opposite to the elite guard of the commander-in-chief, the best unit of which was composed of shield-bearers exclusively (without archers). The Persians were therefore 2.5 times stronger in this location. On the flanks, the Achaemenids tended to place units of lesser combat value, often lightly armed and protected by little more than field fortifications in the form of fences made of *sparā* shields which were tied together and supported on poles. The strike of reinforced Athenian and Plataean hoplites, twelve rows strong, must have had a devastating effect.

The fact that the central divisions actually broke through the Greek lines did not have the catastrophic effect the Persian commanders expected. The Hellenes on the flanks not only held their ground but also moved forward, pushing the Achaemenid right wing into the marshes. Here the Achaemenids resisted a short time (the *tropaion* was later situated in

this spot), hoping to withdraw to the ships before the Greeks attacking the left flank cut off their retreat. The force of the Greek attack pushed most of the Achaemenid soldiers into the marshes. Weighed down by their weapons and not knowing the paths, the invading infantry must have drowned en masse in the bog. The collapse of the Persian left flank resulted in even worse consequences however...

Hoplites of the Ajantis *phyle* on the right wing must have fought in a position that the Achaemenids wanted to defend the most, because it guarded their retreat to the ships. The attacking Greeks managed to push the enemy into the bottleneck of ground between the beach and the marshes. Moreover, the victorious Persian center suddenly found itself at the back of the charging Greek hoplites who had just decimated their left flank, and seeing themselves cut off from the ships, decided to move back (presumably from the area later marked by the *Soros*)

Further reading
- N.Sekunda, *The Persian Army 560-330 BC*. London 1992.
- N.Sekunda, *Marathon*. Oxford 2002.
- D.Head, *The Achaemenid Persian Army*. Stockport 1992.
- P.Briant, *From Cyrus to Alexander. A history of the Persian Empire*. Winona Lake 2002.
- K. Farrokh, *Shadows in the Desert. Ancient Persia at War*. Oxford 2007.

Dress and equipment on the Persian side
The enemy through Greek eyes

The selection of appropriate illustrative material is an extremely difficult task facing any author who takes up the task of writing an account of an ancient battle. This is above all true in the case of the battles fought during the Persian Wars. Only a little more than a decade separates Marathon from the major land battles of the Great Persian War (Thermopylae, Plataea and then after that Mykale). How does one distinguish generic scenes of conflict between Persians and Greeks from specific pictorial references to specific battles? The temptation is to repeat the same images in treatments of separate battles.

By Nicholas Sekunda

Fortunately for us, the Athenians, who were present at all three of the four major battles, still maintained the practice of decorating their vases with detailed pictorial representations when the technique had largely died out in the rest of the Greek world. Athenian vase-paintings remain our principal source of evidence. Our most interesting example, which almost certainly depicts the Battle of Marathon, is the so-called Oxford Brygos cup in the Ashmolean Museum, Oxford.

The Oxford Brygos cup
Greek vases are named in an irregular fashion, which has emerged over the past century and a half. The names of a few potters who signed their products with the short label 'X made this' (*epoiesen*) and the names of an even smaller number of painters 'X painted this' (*egrapsen*) are known from their notices painted on the vases. The cup in the Ashmolean Museum, Oxford, bears the signature of Brygos as potter. The anonymous painter who normally decorated the pots produced by Brygos is known as 'The Brygos Painter', but this cup in Oxford is an exception, decorated in a recognizably different style to the pots normally painted by the 'Brygos Painter'. To differentiate the painter of the Oxford cup from the other, he is known as the 'Oxford Brygos Painter'.

The Oxford Brygos cup contains a wealth of pictorial information concern-

© Nicholas Sekunda

The Oxford Brygos Cup is in the Ashmolean Museum in Oxford. It seems to have been painted after Marathon but before Plataea.

ing the troops fighting on the Persian side at Marathon. It is possible that this fascinating piece of evidence is based on some pictorial or written records made after the battle. The expeditionary force that the Athenians had sent earlier to aid in the Ionian Revolt had given a number of soldiers the opportunity to examine the equipment and dress used by the Persians. We are also told that the Spartans arrived too late to take part in the Battle but

© Nicholas Sekunda

The cup has the signature of the potter, Brygos epoiesen, "Brygos made this", painted under the handle.

© Nicholas Sekunda

The moment in the battle when the Greek hoplite charge meets the Persian shield-wall is shown in this detail from the Oxford Brygos cup.

were present afterwards. According to Herodotus: "Though they had come too late for the battle, they were nevertheless anxious to see the Medes; and so they went to Marathon and saw." (6.120) It is possible that they made some sketches of the equipment and clothing of the dead. Otherwise, the painter was perhaps an eyewitness of the events of the battle.

In the opinion of Williams (1986), it is the battle of Marathon which is specifically shown on the Oxford Brygos Cup, painted in the decade after Marathon, but before Plataea. Three other Attic cups are also placed within the same chronological time-frame by Williams, but these are less

certain to refer to Marathon. In one case, oriental horse-archers are shown in combat with hoplites, an event which is known to have taken place at Plataea, but not at Marathon. In another, a wall of shields is shown, which is remarked on by Herodotus in the case of Plataea, but not at Marathon. The style of the Oxford Brygos Cup seems more archaic than the other vases in the list of Williams, and it is the only one to show the bull as a shield device. The subjugation of the Marathonian bull was one of the labours of Herakes, and after the battle the shield device of a bull, or a bull's head, was used as a method of 'labeling' a warrior who had fought at that

battle – a *Marathonomachos*. Hence the Oxford Brygos Cup is by far and away the most likely candidate to show the battle of Marathon.

Forces on the Persian side

The subtitle of this contribution is carefully selected. One of the remarkable features in the growth of the Persian Empire, is how few ethnic Persians managed to dominate so populous a land mass. Xenophon (*Cyropaedia* 1.2.15) tells us that there were 120,000 Persians. Presumably he has free adult males in mind. The empire over which they held sway has been estimated to number between fifteen and twenty million people. Consequently, the Persians employed mercenaries of various nationalities to fight their wars for them, and the Marathon campaign is unlikely to have been an exception.

In my 2002 book on the battle I suggested that the commander of the expedition, Datis, may have been called 'the Mede' by Herodotus, because he was 'based' in Media – that is, he either held lands in that country, or was its satrap. It is possible, therefore, that his troops were levied in that country. Certainly Ctesias (18) says that the fleet commanded by Datis was 'Median', though Greek sources often use this word as a synonym for Persian.

It is unlikely that ethnic Persians themselves fought at the battle, other than in the role of commanders and small units of 'bodyguards' attached to the latter for their personal defence. One might expect that the person of Datis himself would have been defended by such a unit. Troops acting as bodyguards in the Achaemenid army are called "spear-bearers": *doryphoroi* in Greek and something like *arštibarai* in Old Persian. The army was organized into units of a thousand men, known as a *hazarabam*. The award of a bodyguard was a mark of personal favour by the king. Herodotus (6.113) mentions that the centre of the Persian line at Marathon was held by the best troops: the Persians themselves and the Saka. These 'Persians' are likely to have been a *hazarabam* of spear-bearers. We hear of guards of a thousand Persian spear-bearers defending Oroites the Persian satrap of Lydia during the early part of the reign of Darius (Herodotus 3.127-8). Pausanias the Spartan, after he passed over to Persian service following the battle of Plataea, maintained a

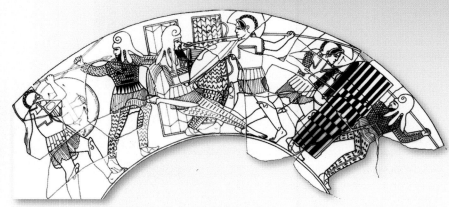

copyright M. C. Miller

This drawing of the outside of the Oxford Brygos Cup, showing several of the Athenian hoplites fighting Persian soldiers. Note that large parts of the cup have been restored.

Sassanid shield lost in fighting that took place in a siege-tunnel cut during the siege of Dura-Europos in AD 257. This complete example is in New Haven, CT.

bodyguard of Egyptian and Median spear-bearers (Thucydides 1.130.1). There were presumably two or three *hazarabam* of Saka mercenaries present at the battle of Marathon as well.

Dress

We know that Persians, Saka, and other nationalities were fighting at Marathon, so it is impossible to establish the ethnic identity of the figures on the Oxford Brygos cup with certainty. Three soldiers fighting on the Persian side are shown on the cup. They wear sleeved tunics and trousers, made of leather or felt, highly decorated with applied bands of material in different colours. The sleeves generally have a ribbon of material stitched to the forward and rear seam. The rest of the sleeve is then decorated with bands of material stitched onto it, either horizontally in wavy or straight bands, or vertically in stripes. Sometimes the two sleeves

are decorated differently, sometimes the same. The sleeves are finished off with a little roll at the cuff.

Trousers are decorated similarly. A dark coloured band of material runs up the front and back of each leg, presumably running along a seam. Sometimes the band of material runs along the outside of the leg, like piping along the seams of 19th century military trousers. The areas of trouser demarcated by these vertical seams are sometimes left plain, and sometimes decorated by sewn-on horizontal bands, either wavy or straight. The trousers worn by the best-preserved figure on the cup are decorated with stitched appliqué patches of darker coloured material in a diamond or irregular leaf-shape pattern.

A view of the headgear is only fully preserved on one of the figures. He is wearing a 'Persian hood' with a rounded lobe flopping over at the front and five lappets hanging over the sides and the back. The Persian hood with five lappets is non-standard in Greek art, and suggests that the artist is following sources specific for Marathon.

A view of the boots is also only present in the fully-preserved figure. Here the boots are tied by wrapping flaps of leather around the ankle. These would end in lace-type thongs, which would be knotted somewhat higher up the ankle. The knot is obscured by the trousers. The boots would probably be of an un-dyed tan colour, though surviving paintings show Persian boots dyed yellow, red or even blue.

The wicker shield

A view of the wicker shield, the *spara*, is preserved in its entirety in the hand of one of the figures on the cup, although a view of a second is partially preserved. The wicker shield was called *gerrhon* in the Greek sources, and Achaemenid troops bearing wicker shields of this type *gerrhophoroi*. The equivalent terms can be established in Old Persian thanks to a gloss preserved in the lexicon of Hesychius (s.v. *sparabara*) where he tells us that the word is equivalent to the Greek *gerrhophoroi* "bearers of wicker shields." The information supplied by Hesychius in this gloss is probably derived from the lost history of Ctesias of Knidos, who was a doctor at the Persian Court during the reign of Artaxerxes II and who tended to 'spice' his account by the rendition of Old Persian terminology. The validity of the informa-

tion supplied by Hesychius is supported by the survival of the word *ispar* as one of the words used for "shield" into Middle and New Persian.

The *spara*-shield was constructed by weaving osiers in and out of holes that had been made in a large (typically rectangular) piece of rawhide. When the rawhide dried out and contracted, it put the osiers under tension. The osiers were thus flexed and the whole shield construction was strengthened. This combination of materials put under tension resulted in a shield of great lightness yet of great resilience. The osiers and the rawhide could be dyed or painted in several different colours, and the osiers were frequently woven through the rawhide in such a way as to give a V- or W-shaped pattern.

Fighting-spears were also used by the *sparabara*. The standard formation adopted by Achaemenid infantry was in a file ten ranks deep. The *sparabara* were certainly stationed in the first rank, were they drew their wicker shields up into a wall. Walls of wicker shields are mentioned by Herodotus at Plataea (9.61) and Mykale (9.99, 102) though not, strangely, at Marathon. It seems that the "decurions" (*daθapatiš*) in the first rank of a Persian infantry file carried wicker shields,

Another shield from Dura, now in New Haven, CT, here viewed from the inside, has only survived in fragmentary condition, but the central wooden handle of the shield is clearly demonstrated, as is the construction of the shield as a whole

and, like medieval pavise-bearers, protected the archers who made up the rest of the unit. It seems that the archers who formed the remaining nine lines of the decury would not carry the wicker shield, although we cannot be certain of this fact. Presumably, the archers carried swords too, but only the decurions in the first rank carried fighting-spears as well.

The composite cuirass

The cuirasses worn by all the three figures shown fighting on the Persian side are of the type known as 'composite' to Greek archaeologists. But they differ from Greek cuirasses of this type in significant details. The cuirass worn by the best-preserved of the figures is decorated with a pattern of diagonal lines criss-crossing the cuirass and dividing it into lozenge shapes. The small dots in the centre of the lozenges could represent rivets holding bronze plates between surface layers of leather on the inside and outside of the cuirass; while the diagonal lines may represent stitching. Therefore, this could represent the ancient equivalent of a Medieval 'jack' or 'brigantine'. A line of groin-flaps is attached at the bottom. These seem to be of stiff leather, deliberately split into 'tassels' at the bottom to prevent them chafing the thighs.

On the representation of the second soldier shown in Persian service from the Oxford Brygos cup, the section of the cuirass guarding the front of the trunk is covered with a layer of leather decorated with a lozenge pattern. As I have suggested elsewhere in this issue, this could have been influenced by the pattern of scales, which came into use at this time alongside armour that was constructed from a series of plates of diverse materials. Both side-plates are shown, made of scales of leather or bronze, or more probably iron, sewn onto a stiff base and left uncovered. The shoulder plates are also made of scales with rounded ends, bound at the edge with a leather band. The groin-flaps are rectangular metal plates with curved ends of the normal type, but covered with leather, painted half white and half black with a diagonal border. Under the groin-flaps, he wears a garment which seems to be an apron of pleated material wrapped around the groin for extra protection, rather that a tunic. It is decorated with a single dark line running parallel to the edge.

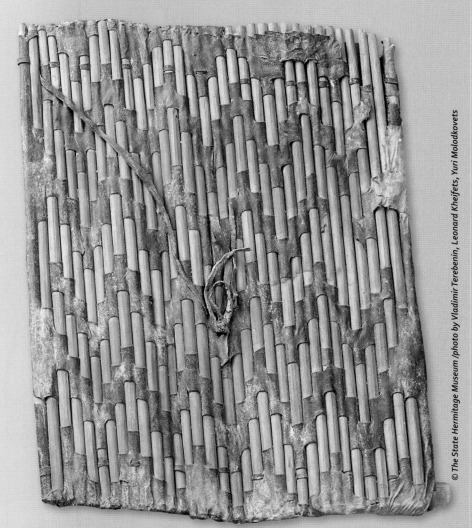

© The State Hermitage Museum /photo by Vladimir Terebenin, Leonard Kheifets, Yuri Molodkovets

Shield from a Pazyryk tomb in Siberia belonging to some local tribal chief. The tomb was cut into the permafrost which explains the excellent state of preservation of the organic objects found there. The dating of the tomb is subject to considerable controversy, but perhaps a date near the end of the third century would be appropriate. The tomb contains a number of items imported from the Achaemenid world. To judge from its size, the Pazyryk shield was probably used by a cavalrymen. Now in the State Hermitage Museum, St. Petersburg, Russia.

© New Haven, Yale University Art Gallery, New Haven: Dura Europos Collection

Different versions of the wicker shield were carried by the infantry and the cavalry. Infantry shields are large and rectangular, while cavalry shields are smaller, and could be of more varied shape. The size of the Dura shields, as well as the shape, suggests that these shields were designed to be used by cavalry. This is suggestively demonstrated in this archive photograph of the Dura excavations, featuring the same shield as in the first illustration.

The cuirass worn by the third figure fighting on the Persian side bears more resemblance to composite cuirasses normally worn by Greeks: it is almost identical in fact. It is fitted with shoulder-guards and a light coloured chest-plate presumably covered with stiffened leather and decorated with a band of geometric patterning high up on the chest. The side-plates on the cuirass are decorated with a diamond pattern, and the cuirass is fitted with groin-flaps. The composite cuirass only became popular in Greece during the sixth century BC, and it seems highly probable that it is of Near-Eastern origin.

Swords

The type of sword used on the Persian side is only just visible in the hands of the third figure shown on the Oxford Brygos cup. It can be identified as a type known to Greeks as a *kopis* or *machaira*. *Kopis* is a word connected with the Greek verb *koptein*, "to chop", and is more suitable for a heavy single-bladed sword of this type, whereas *machaira* is a more general word applied to a whole range of swords and knives. The *kopis* swords were rather like machetes in appearance, with iron blades slightly curving towards the tip on the outside, without guards, and with a handle consisting of two plates of wood or stone fixed to either side of the iron blade. Xenophon (*Cyropaedia* 1.2.9, 13) lists the *kopis* (or the *sagaris* "battle-axe") among the weapons normally carried by the Persians. They would be held in a scabbard of two wooden boards fixed together and covered in leather. Scabbards are often omitted from painted Greek vases.

Cavalry

The Persian expeditionary force that landed at Marathon almost certainly included a force of cavalry, commanded by Artaphernes 'the Younger', son of Artaphernes the elder, who was brother

This plate shows the Persian forces as they landed in the Bay of Marathon (background). The cavalry has safely arrived, having disembarked from their horse transports. The ethnic affiliation of this cavalryman, inspired on the Faina cup, is not known, the slightly different hat, for example, suggest a different heritage. The infantrymen are both sparabara, *armed with large wicker shields and spears.*

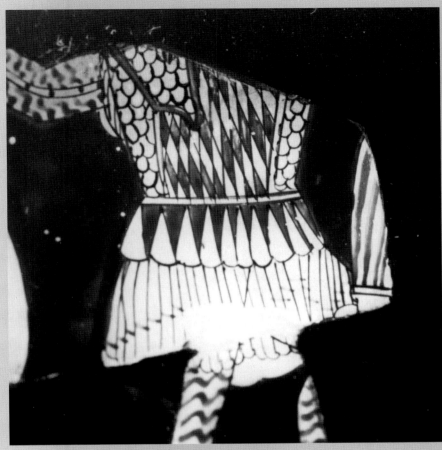

Second figure showing a warrior fighting on the Persian side on the Oxford Brygos cup, wearing body armour covered in a lozenge pattern.

of Darius and satrap in Sardis. Pausanias (1.32.7) mentions the "mangers of the horses of Artaphernes" carved in the rocks at Marathon, which suggests that Artaphernes commanded the cavalry. Following the Marathon campaign, he accompanied Datis back to Susa with the Eretrian prisoners (Herodotus 6.119). He later took part in the second Persian campaign against Greece in 480, commanding one of the army contingents (Herodotus 7.74). Herodotus in his account of the battle does not make mention of this cavalry, but he mentions that the Persian fleet included horse-transports (6.95): the first time ships of this type are mentioned. The riders presumably sailed in the same ships as their steeds.

A Greek proverb is mentioned in a Byzantine lexicon. This lexicon was thought at one time to have been compiled by an individual named Suidas. The name on the title page was subsequently thought to be a reference to the place the lexicon was compiled in: the Suda monastery in Crete. This explanation fails to convince,

however, because Suidas is a perfectly respectable personal name, given to a succession of Thessalian bishops. Anyway, in this lexicon, under the entry *Chōris Hippeis* ("The Cavalry are away") we read:

"Datis having invaded Attica, they say that the Ionians on his going back went up to the trees and made signs to the Athenians that the cavalry were away; and Miltiades on becoming aware of their withdrawal engaged on those terms and was victorious. That is why the proverb is used of those who break formation."

This explains the absence of any cavalry from the Persian side at the battle. Presumably they had already been embarked aboard the horse-transports to sail to Athens. The Ionians mentioned in this passage of Suidas would have been

individuals forced into Persian service and accompanying the Persian fleet. The 'trees' mentioned in the passage may be a reference to the sacred grove by the Herakleion where the Athenian and Plataean forces were encamped.

The saying has been restored – only the first three letters are still legible – by Williams, in the caption of an Attic cup in Orvieto, once in the Faina Collection (no. 48) showing a horse-archer in oriental clothing. The cup had originally been attributed to Onesimos but Williams preferred to attribute it to the Antiphon Painter. Either way, it is perfectly possible that the cup was painted in the aftermath of Marathon, and if the restoration of Williams is sound, we cannot escape the conclusion that one of Artaphernes' cavalrymen is being shown.

The figure is shown wearing a hat similar to that being worn on the Oxford Brygos cup, but not identical. The hat has the same five lappets, but the bowl of the hat is sharply delineated from these. Blotchy shading indicates the material the hat is made from, either fur or felt, and the bowl itself ends in a tiny but distinct point. The rider is heavily bearded. He wears a composite cuirass viewed from the back. The shoulder-guards are decorated on the back with a single four-pointed star with a dot in the centre. The four points of the star are displayed in the position of a saltire (Saint Andrews' cross). The body of the cuirass is decorated above the waist with a line of eight large dots, and the groin-flaps below the waist reflect this and are decorated with a large single dot too. The sleeves of his tunic are decorated with a series of stripes of light coloured material, presumably they are sewn onto a dark coloured background. These stripes are running parallel to the seam. The seam itself is decorated with a stripe of light coloured material decorated with a series of small dark spots. The cuffs end it a little roll decorated with a line of light coloured dots. Over this sleeved tunic, he wears a second tunic of crinkly linen, which is visible under the right shoulder-guard and the groin-flaps. The horseman wears trousers

In this plate Persian infantry is retreating off the battlefield to their destruction in the Great Marsh that lay behind their lines.

A third oriental fighting on the Persian side falls beneath the charge of a Greek hoplite. The bottom of a bull's head is visible on the hoplite shield in the centre of the fragment. Beneath the hoplite shield is the spara *(shield) of the Persian. The cuirass is identical to the type of composite cuirass used by Greeks. Just visible is an apron wrapped round his waist under the groin-flaps. Note the fine beard.*

with the front seam decorated with a thin band of material covered in small dots. This band is continued around the bottom edge of the trousers. The main body of the trousers is decorated with bands of zigzag lines running horizontally, alternating with rows of elongated heart shapes. The boots appear to be of leather ending in a triangular shaped extension wrapped several times around the instep.

In his right hand, the mounted archer holds a bow, apparently of a shape used by the Scythians and their Asian Saka cousins. This was distinguished by its shape, as it resembled the Greek letter *sigma* and had a lower ear slightly shorter than the upper ear, thus enabling it to be shot more easily from horseback. A bow-case is hung at the horseman's right side below the belt. We do not know to what ethnic group the horseman represented on the Faina cup would have belonged, but the probability must be that he is a Saka. These nomadic horsemen were much in favour as mercenaries by the Achemenids. ●

Nicholas Sekunda has published many books and articles about warfare and warriors of the Ancient world. He currently teaches at the Institute of Archaeology, Gdansk, Poland.

Further reading
- A.A. Barrett, M.J. Vickers, 'The Oxford Brygos cup reconsidered', in: *Journal of Hellenic Studies* 98 (1978) 17-24.
- N.V. Sekunda, 'Achaemenid Military Terminology', in: *Archäologische Mitteilungen aus Iran* 21 (1988) 69-77.
- D. Williams, 'A cup by the Antiphon Painter and the Battle of Marathon', in: *Studien zur Mythologie und Vasenmalerei Konrad Schauenburg.* Mainz am Rhein 1986, p.75-81.

War and public monuments in ancient Greece
Remembering Marathon

Even though Marathon was only one of many battles fought during what became known as the Greco-Persian Wars, it has always been treated as an especially glorious victory in European history. And even in recent historical publications for the wider public one still finds Marathon defined as the "historical salvation of the cradle of Western civilisation".

By Natascha Sojc

In his detailed and thrilling account, the Greek historian Herodotus described how a small number of Athenians triumphed over the more numerous Persians while defending their homeland. Because Herodotus' history, this most famous of sources for the battle, is literary, many of his readers through the ages seem to have felt the need to find support in the material realm for his claim of a glorious Greek victory. This is attested to, for example, by a 19th century painting by Carl Rottmann, where the glory of the victory is presented as a wild landscape under a vast sky, a thunderstorm retreating into distance. In that same period, elements of weaponry brought home from Greece as souvenirs catered to the same need: to make the Battle of Marathon something 'real', something one could visualize and touch.

But nowadays one can ask instead how the battle of Marathon came to be considered this one, decisive victory. How were the traumatic aspects of war - blood, wounds and death - transformed into a mark in history? To answer these questions one has to turn to archaeological sources, which can be traced back to the time immediately after the battle. In other words, sources that predate the account in Herodotus' history. The Marathon monuments differ in form as well as content and they were erected over a period of time longer than one generation. They point to a development from monument to memorial: the 'materialized memory' of war went through different phases and accordingly the aspects that should be remembered or even forgotten changed in the course of time.

First phase: after the battle

The first Marathon monuments were constructed just after the battle and were linked directly to the realities of the event itself. For instance, in the tumulus still visible today on the plain of Marathon, Greek warriors are presumed to have been buried. This allows us to assume that the soldiers who fell on the battlefield were not buried individually and that their relationship to their combat unit took precedence over family or other social ties. This type of burial also determined how the dead were commemorated: it can be assumed that, from that point on, those who fell at Marathon were collectively remembered on the occasion of an annual festival in honour of some deity. Furthermore the tomb for the fallen Greeks on the field of Marathon represented the events of that war by honouring its victims. With regard to the question at hand, it can be ascertained that the violent events related to the experience of war were already partially transformed into a monument directly after the battle: the dead were buried on the battlefield and were thus consigned to a second – 'symbolic' – death in the form of their burial tumulus. Conversely, the Persians who were killed, as later Roman sources report, were buried in an unmarked mass grave. The remains of the enemy were thus not used to symbolise something, but the Greeks instead consigned them to obscurity.

After the battle the Athenians collected the weapons that had either been abandoned or belonged to the enemy dead. Some of the items obtained in this manner were subsequently used in the context of making a sacrificial offering to the gods by erecting a symbol of victory, a so-called *tropaion*. *Tropaia* were traditionally made of wooden frames onto which the spoils were nailed. In a simpler version, *tropaia* took the form of a pile of weapons. On the battlefield the *tropaion* was either erected where the battle began or where the course of a war took a fortunate turn. Hence, the weapons that were actually used in the battle, which were both valuable metal objects and a means of exercising force, were diverted from their intended use and put together to form a 'monument'. It was direct proof of victory and an offering to gods which allowed them to participate in the spoils. Such a monument gives rise to numerous associations: the enemy is now unprotected, robbed of his weapons and the weapons will no longer pose a threat. Because the *tropaion* was erected directly on the battlefield, the 'monument' maintained a direct connection to the actual battle, which in this way was also maintained in the memories of the contemporaries.

While the existence of a *tropaion* on the plain of Marathon, i.e. on the battlefield itself, can only be postulated and determined in a general manner by means of archaeological finds, it can be assumed that there was at least one more *tropaion*, which was also dedicated immediately after the Battle of Marathon, this one in a sanctuary. Finds unearthed at the extensive sanctuary of Zeus in Olympia (where not only temple buildings where located but where the Olympic Games were also held, where all Greek city-states participated in religious rituals) seem to have belonged to a Marathon *tropaion* that commemorated this battle. In addition to a scattering of spearheads and quiver fittings, nearly fifty trefoil arrowheads were found. Some of these exhibit evidence of having been bent on impact. A conical

Private vessels for wine drinking, contemporary with the painting of the Stoa Poikile showed similar battle scenes with sterotype Greeks winning over equally stereotype Persians. Drawing of a Attic redfigure drinking vessel (whereabouts unknown – published E. Gerhard, Auserlesene griechische Vasenbilder III (1847) table 166.).

© *Public domain*

helmet was also found: the inscription incised into the helmet tells us that the Athenians had taken it from the Persians and were now dedicating it to Zeus. The evidence of a victory at Marathon was therefore represented in the sanctuary of Zeus at Olympia through the dedication of weaponry, mainly attack weapons, to form a *tropaion*. At the same time, both the Athenian city state and individuals gave thanks to the highest deity in this manner, paid their due to the god and thanked him for his support. Symbolically, some part of the battle was put into his hands and at the same time, a direct reminder of a violent conflict was established.

The Athenian Marathon *tropaion* probably erected in the region of the stadium's finish line must have held a very prominent place in this sanctuary. Especially during the Olympic games when the different Greek city states' athletes competed against each other, the *tropaion* was there on public display for all fellow Greeks to admire what spoils the Athenians had taken from the Persians. And at the same time they were impressed or even intimidated by the capability of the Athenian fighting force, as in this period Greek city-states might also get involved in combat against each other.

Second phase: veiling realities

During the second phase of Marathon monuments abstraction set in. This means that the event of war was no longer embedded in the monuments' formal representation, but was instead transformed into a monumentalised memorial.

In the 1960s, ancient spoils were recovered that had been built into a medieval structure erected on the plain of Marathon. They were presumably part of the marble Marathon *tropaion* the Roman traveller Pausanias writes about (*Guide for Greece* 1.32.4). It was possible to reconstruct a column measuring ten metres (see p.36) which would originally have been crowned by the goddess of victory, a striding Nike, similar to the one familiar to us from later *tropaia* of this type.

What does this tell us about how monuments provided the Athenians of that period with a means of coming to terms with a military altercation? The replacement of the *tropaion* consisting of weaponry erected immediately after the Battle of Marathon with a stone monument at a later date is the first example of this practice in Greek culture. It is also notable that its outer appearance had nothing to do with the real violence of the military action. While the weapons of the first *tropaion* were material proof of a victory, here it is the sculptural figure of Nike, the image of the goddess on the stone monument that attests to the victory. The direct references to the military action have disappeared, masked by a perfect marble column that obscures the details of the event. On the basis of parallels in Ionic-Attic architecture the Marathon monument can be dated either one or two decades after the Battle of Marathon. Obviously the Athenians felt that a monument consisting of weapons and equipment was no longer needed as proof of their victory and that there was instead a need for a proper 'memorial', a piece of art where a statue of Nike, and thereby the goddess of victory herself, was presented as witness of the victory.

But victory, personified in a figure of the goddess, was not the only abstract concept brought into association with the Battle of Marathon. The Athenians used another part of the profits of the spoils from Marathon to make an offering to the god Apollo in the diety's sanctuary at Delphi, famous for its oracle venerated by all Greek city-states. Next to the Athenian treasury, which was completed in roughly 500 BC, a base was added. It bore a now fragmentary inscription referring to the

battle. This base, as the many indentations show, may originally have carried weapons captured by the Athenians in battle, i.e. it was another Marathon *tropaion*. Later this first offering was substituted with up to sixteen statues, thereby becoming one of the most extensive and costly offerings in this sanctuary. Among the figures were the deities and mythical heroes of the city of Athens and also the ten mythical kings of Attica, who were depicted as idealised male figures. These mythical kings, also called *phyle*-heroes, personified the ten eponymous Attic tribes into which the citizens of Athens were organised after Cleisthenes' democratic reforms some years before the Greco-Persian wars – a reform which was approved by Apollo's oracle.

While in later times, depictions of the ten *phyle*-heroes became a common and potent formula for the Athenian citiziens' collective, in Delphi, where they were probably displayed for the first time, they have a special connection to the Battle of Marathon. Within this context, the *phyle*-heroes seem to primarily symbolize the

troops of the individual tribes who came together to form the Attic army in the battle. The fighting force is not depicted here as the mass of men, but rather as the sum of ten brigades. During the battle, they acted as independent tactical units, each led by its own general. This is reported by the historian Herodotus, who recognized this principle, which was used to organise the fighting force, as a decisive key to the victory over the Persians.

On the Marathon monument in Delphi, the *phyle*-heroes represent the 'battle collective' in idealised form and they honour it at the same time. It can be presumed that even individual warriors who participated in the battle identified with these *phyle*-heroes. However, this offering is also justifiably seen as a memorial with a concrete message addressed to the other Greek city-states: it served to demonstrate that the new political order in Athens, democracy, guaranteed its military power and was favoured by the gods.

Last phase: pathos and propaganda
In a third phase of Marathon monuments, which were erected approximately one generation after the event, the battle is represented in a narrative, historical manner. This appears to be the concluding stage in the process of coming to terms with the battle through public works. And

Funerary urn depicting the myth of the man with the plough: during the battle, a man was seen slaying many Persians using a ploughshare. When the Athenians looked for him after the battle, he could not be found. An oracle then commanded them to worship Echetlaeus (the hero with the echetlon, the plough), who was also depicted on the painting in the Stoa Polike.

it is only at this stage that a political usage of the battle as 'glorious Athenian victory' becomes apparent. In the 460s, i.e. well after the Greco-Persian Wars, a structure was built on the Athenian Agora, in the political centre of the city, where assemblies where held and laws and decrees where made public. There the so-called *Stoa Poikile* ("Painted Stoa") was newly erected, a building closed along one of the long sides and open to the Agora on the other. In this hall four paintings, planned as an ensemble from the outset and ordered by the people's assembly, were exhibited for public viewing. These paintings are known to us only from the descriptions found in classical literary sources (e.g. Pausanias) and depicted various battles, including the Battle of Marathon.

The first painting in the series showed the Athenian army marching off to battle. We know nothing more specific about this painting today. It was followed by two images of mythical battles: the battle of the Athenians against the Amazons and a scene from the Trojan War. The gallery was completed by the painting of the Battle of Marathon which depicted the course of the battle. It showed the Athenians leaving the camp they had established on the plain of Marathon, in the temple district of the hero Heracles. Aided by a brigade from Plataea, they determinedly march against the enemy. Next, and particularly prominent in the picture, are the individual clashes between Greeks and fleeing Persians, in man-to-man combat. As the last phase of the battle, the pictures show the flight of the Persians, initially in hasty retreat through the swamps and finally attempting to embark their ships. Various superhuman figures can be seen in the painting as well, including Athena and mythical heroes such as Heracles and Theseus: they support the Athenians in battle with their powers. In addition, a number of 'renowned Athenians' can be recognised in the picture and are spotlighted in the battle scenes, mainly generals. The general Miltiades is depicted as providing the Greeks encouragement in the opening phase of the battle and another strategist, Kynegeiros, is attempting to prevent a Persian ship from fleeing, which ultimately leads to his arm being severed by a Persian wielding an axe. Thus the painting not only depicts the phases of the battle and the intercession of superhuman forces, but also feats of heroism by individual historical figures, like an otherwise unknown Athenian who had impressed the other fighters with the bravery he and his bloodhound had displayed during battle.

Hence, the Marathon painting is considered the first historical painting in classical Antiquity. Remarkably, it was created perhaps a decade before Herodotus's historical work in which the individual episodes of the battle are described in a similar manner. Thus, another Athenian, Epizelus, who was blinded in the battle after he allegedly saw a giant fighting on the side of the Persians, is not only depicted in the painting, his story is also related by Herodotus, who claims to have heard the story first-hand.

The painting in the *Stoa Poikile* is the first time that the violent struggle, combat, injury and death related to the Battle of Marathon were depicted in the public sphere, and it undoubtedly gave rise to emotional reactions on the part of the viewers (which is also attested by later literary sources). This had never previously been the case with regard to the monuments and other sources related to the Battle of Marathon. Exhibited alongside images of mythical battles, the battle of Marathon was now so far removed from the present that it could be represented as a violent event through the medium of painting. Even an arch-enemy was now defined by it, the Persian. From then on allusions to Marathon in the public sphere (and even on Hellenistic-era Etruscan urns and Roman sarcophagi) refer back to the dramatic and bloody representation of Marathon in the *Stoa Poikile*. The Marathon painting can, therefore, also be considered as a final step in the public process of coming to terms with the event itself. Furthermore the painting in the *Stoa Poikile* clearly represents the first instance in which the Battle of Marathon was used for political gain: with the emotional reaction it provoked in contemporaries, it could be used to motivate the citizenry for the city's new military campaigns. Exhibited at the centre of political life, no longer connected to a sanctuary or dedicated to a god, it glorified the Athenian military deeds, made heroes out of the Athenian warriors and gave a clearly recognizable face to the enemy par excellence. In the *Stoa Poikile* painting it seems that the military events of Marathon were constructed for the first time as the glori-

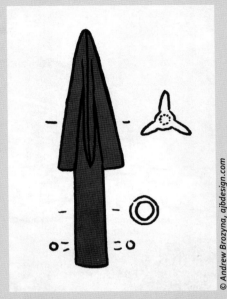

Persian spearhead. An example of the offensive weapons collected after the battle of Marathon by the Athenians and then dedicated into the sanctury of Zeus at Olympia. After Baitinger.

© Andrew Brozyna, ajbdesign.com

ous historic victory and potent salvation it is still considered nowadays.●

Professor Natascha Sojc was recently installed as Byvanck professor of Classical Archaeology at the University of Leiden, the Netherlands. This is an abbreviated version of her inaugural lecture. She would like to express her thanks to Maureen Roycroft Sommer for revisions in an earlier English version of this text.

Further reading:
- H. Baitinger, 'Waffen und Bewaffnungen aus der Perserbeute in Olympia', in: *Archäologischer Anzeiger* 1999, 125-139.
- H.R. Goette and T. M. Weber, *Marathon. Siedlungskammer und Schlachtfeld – Sommerfrische und olympische Wettkampfstätte.* Mainz 2004.
- M. Jung, *Marathon und Plataiai: zwei Perserschlachten als "lieux de mémoire" im antiken Griechenland.* Göttingen 2006.

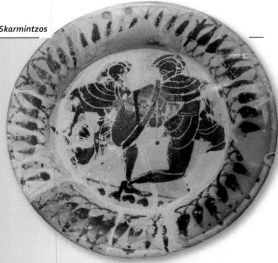

Plate depicting hoplites from the early 5th century BC. From the excavated tombs at Marathon.

Tips for visiting the area
At the tomb of Marathon and beyond

Two and a half thousand years have passed since the Battle of Marathon. Though the accuracy of that dating is a matter of debate, the fact remains that the battle between a city-state and an empire produced a rather unlikely outcome: the city-state won. The battle became a landmark to those who would struggle against empires in the future and provided proof that determined men can stand against all odds and prevail.

By Stefanos Skarmintzos

Lovers of history have made pilgrimages to the site of this battle, though it was hidden in the mists of time and now hardly matches the description of Herodotus. Houses, farms and even an Olympic Class Rowing facility now stand upon it. The people of modern Athens enjoy swimming on the beach where Kynegeiros was killed. So what can the history lover or military enthusiast find here? Please indulge your guide who is more of a history lover than a tourist group leader.

Marathon is located on the east coast of Attica. All hotels there are usually fully booked with Athenians on vacation or foreign tourists and are reputed to be expensive for what they offer. If your objective is the battle site and everything relating to it, you stand a better chance finding a hotel located in the city of Athens. Moreover, none of the items of interest relating to the battle of Marathon are in the Marathon Museum!

A good collection of weapons, marbles and pottery may be found in the National Archaeological Museum. It is located in the center of Athens and easily accessible by public transport. Of course, everyone who visits Athens wants to visit the Acropolis, but military enthusiasts will want to see some of the items in the Acropolis Museum (which requires a different ticket), which date to the era of the Persian Wars. With the ticket bought at the Acropolis you can also visit the Agora Museum. There you can see the metal exterior of a Spartan shield, pottery with interesting military scenes and the *ostraca* bearing the names of the generals who led Athens during the Persian Wars and were subsequently exiled by their fellow citizens! For more weapons and related gear, reconstructions included, go to the War Museum. That'll also show you that Greece has more history besides the Persian Wars!

When the Big Day comes and you're off to Marathon, take the KTEL bus service. It is very affordable and starts close to the National Archaeological Museum. Get off at the Vranas bus stop and inquire for the Museum of Marathon. Don't expect to find much Archaic or classical Greek stuff there. Most items have to do with the Roman era, such as the shrine of Isis and the villa of Herodes Atticus. You may also want to visit the tomb of Marathon. To be honest, there isn't much to see there either except an earthen hillock and a modern statue of Miltiades along with a plaque bearing Simonides inscription "while defending Greeks, Athenians smashed the might of gold-decorated Persians."

Yet the more precious items related to the battle are not even in Attica. Those who can afford an excursion to Olympia (money-wise or time-wise) will have the chance to see a Persian helmet of 'babylonian type' and (reportedly) Miltiades' helmet with the inscription dedicating it to Zeus by a grateful general. Readers from the UK might want to know that in the British Museum there are a few items from the tomb of Marathon as well.

The Marathon tomb is worth a visit for those who enjoy reflecting on the past, but the Museums are where the tangible side can be found of the times that marked not only Greek, but global history as well. ●

Some advice
- If you can, take a bus or the subway extension from the airport into Athens. Taxis are very expensive.
- Most museums in Athens are close to the Metro Stations.
- Athens is *hot* in Summer. Do not buy water from kiosks near museums or tourist sites. The bottles don't lay there long enough to cool. Better to get your group into a supermarket and buy it there, or get it from kiosks on your way to the site, but don't buy it on site.
- Sometimes hotels offer excursions to archeological sites. It may be worth inquiring about possibilities.
- While touring museums or sites be prepared to do a lot of walking.
- Photos (without flash) are allowed in Athenian museums except in Acropolis Museum.